AI Bas
The Fundamentals

Book One of the NewBits AI Trilogy

This Book Marks the Beginning of Our Journey into the Exciting World of Artificial Intelligence.

We Will Be Demystifying This Transformative Technology, Exploring Everything from Its Evolution and Basic Principles to Its Real-World Applications and Ethical Considerations.

"It's all about the bits...especially the new bits."

GIL OREN

GIL OREN

AI BASICS: THE FUNDAMENTALS

AI Basics: The Fundamentals
Book One of the NewBits AI Trilogy
by Gil Oren

Published by NewBits Media
A Division of NewBits, LLC
newbits.ai
First Edition: 2024
Printed in the United States of America

ISBN: 9798345979853

This is a work of non-fiction. All information presented is believed to be accurate at the time of publication. The author and publisher disclaim any liability in connection with the use of this information.

AI DISCLOSURE
This book was created in collaboration with artificial intelligence. Content was partially generated, edited, and refined using leading AI language models. The author has carefully reviewed, verified, and takes full responsibility for all content. This approach aligns with our mission at NewBits Media, a division of NewBits, LLC, to demonstrate practical applications of AI technology while maintaining high standards of quality and accuracy.

Cover design created with AI assistance.

Some names and identifying details may have been changed to protect the privacy of individuals.

GIL OREN

For Melissa, Zachary, Sydney, Ava, and Dixie

- my everything.

GIL OREN

TABLE OF CONTENTS

GIL OREN

WELCOME TO THE NEWBITS AI TRILOGY

The world of Artificial Intelligence can seem complex and overwhelming. Headlines trumpet AI's latest achievements and potential threats, while businesses rush to adopt AI solutions they may not fully understand. Technical jargon and complex mathematics often create barriers rather than bridges to understanding. Yet in today's rapidly evolving technological landscape, understanding AI isn't just for experts, it's crucial for everyone.

This belief sparked a mission to make AI knowledge truly accessible to all and led to the creation of this trilogy. As the growing divide between AI's increasing influence and people's understanding of it became apparent, it was clear that a different approach to AI education was needed. Not just scattered tutorials or dense academic texts, but a carefully structured journey that builds confidence and competence step by step.

AI Basics: The Fundamentals marks the beginning of our journey together. This first book demystifies core AI concepts, exploring everything from its evolution and basic principles to its real-world applications and ethical considerations. The book is designed to build your foundation in AI, whether you're a curious beginner or a professional seeking deeper understanding. It cuts through the hype and complexity to reveal AI's true nature, a powerful tool that, when properly understood, becomes an enabler rather than an intimidator.

Each chapter has been carefully crafted to build upon the last, ensuring you develop a clear, comprehensive understanding of AI's fundamentals. The book explores not just what AI is, but why it works the way it does, how it's evolving, and what that means for our future. From machine learning basics to ethical considerations, from practical applications to potential pitfalls, you'll gain the knowledge needed to navigate the AI landscape with confidence.

This trilogy represents a carefully crafted progression. From the fundamentals we establish here, we'll move into *AI Toolbox: Empowering the Learner*, where you'll gain hands-on experience with AI tools and technologies. You'll learn not just how to use AI solutions, but how to evaluate them, implement them, and maximize their potential. Finally, in *AI Frontier: Navigating the Cutting Edge*, we'll explore the latest developments and future possibilities of AI, preparing you to be part of the conversation about where AI is heading and how it will shape our world.

The approach throughout is simple yet powerful: break down complex concepts into digestible, engaging content that bridges theory and real-world application. True understanding comes not just from knowing facts, but from seeing how they connect to real-world scenarios and practical applications. Throughout these books, you'll find examples, case studies, and insights that bring AI concepts to life.

This trilogy is more than just a guide, it's the cornerstone of a larger vision. A vision of a world where AI knowledge is accessible to everyone, where understanding technology empowers rather than intimidates, and where learning happens through clear explanation and practical application.

It's about building a community of informed individuals who can confidently engage with AI, whether they're using it, developing it, or making decisions about its implementation.

We're living in a pivotal time in technological history. AI is not just changing how we work; it's transforming how we live, learn, and interact with the world around us. Understanding AI has become as fundamental as understanding the internet at the dawn of the digital age. Through this trilogy, you'll develop not just knowledge, but the critical thinking skills needed to evaluate AI developments and opportunities as they emerge.

Let's begin this journey together, one concept at a time. Welcome to the *NewBits AI Trilogy*.

GIL OREN

CHAPTER 1: INTRODUCTION TO AI BASICS

Picture yourself going through a typical day. Your morning alarm, optimized by AI, wakes you during your lightest sleep phase. As you check your phone, AI algorithms have already curated your news feed, filtered your email spam, and selected social media content tailored to your interests. Your route to work is optimized by AI-powered traffic systems, while your favorite coffee shop's inventory management system, also AI-driven, has ensured your preferred breakfast is in stock.

This isn't a glimpse into the future, it's the reality of today. Artificial Intelligence has woven itself into the fabric of our daily lives, often operating so seamlessly that we barely notice its presence. Yet this ubiquitous technology, for all its everyday applications, represents one of the most profound transformations in human history.

The reach of AI extends far beyond our smartphones and personal devices. In healthcare, AI systems analyze medical images with remarkable accuracy, helping doctors detect diseases earlier and with greater precision. In financial markets, AI algorithms execute millions of trades per second, responding to market changes faster than any human could. In manufacturing, AI-powered robots work alongside humans, learning and adapting to new tasks with increasing sophistication.

The healthcare revolution brought about by AI demonstrates the breadth of its impact. Modern medical facilities employ AI systems that detect early signs of cancer in medical imaging with accuracy rates matching or exceeding human experts. These same facilities use machine learning algorithms to predict patient readmission risks, helping hospitals optimize care. The development of new medications has been dramatically accelerated by AI-powered drug discovery processes, while virtual health assistants now provide round-the-clock initial patient screening and monitoring.

In the business world, the transformation is equally profound. Customer service has evolved with chatbots handling millions of inquiries globally, learning and improving with each interaction. Predictive analytics now forecast market trends, inventory needs, and maintenance requirements with unprecedented accuracy. Companies employ AI-driven recruitment tools to identify promising candidates while reducing bias, and automated accounting systems vigilantly detect fraud patterns and anomalies in real-time.

The entertainment industry, too, has been revolutionized. Streaming services employ sophisticated AI to predict and recommend content, creating personalized experiences for each viewer. Video game worlds have become more immersive, with AI creating realistic character behaviors and dynamic environments that respond to player actions. Even the creative process itself has been enhanced, with AI-generated music assisting composers and creating background scores, while virtual reality systems use AI to create increasingly immersive and responsive experiences.

Yet these visible applications represent merely the tip of the iceberg. Behind the scenes, AI systems monitor and maintain power grids, optimize global shipping routes, and protect against cybersecurity threats. They control smart building systems, manage telecommunications networks, and guide autonomous systems in space exploration. The invisible web of AI influence extends into nearly every aspect of modern infrastructure.

We stand at an inflection point in human history, comparable to the advent of electricity or the internet. Just as those innovations fundamentally altered how societies function, AI is reshaping our world in profound and often unexpected ways.

The pace of AI advancement has been nothing short of extraordinary. Machine learning systems now create art that wins competitions against human artists. Language models engage in sophisticated conversations and assist in creative writing tasks that once seemed exclusively human. AI researchers make breakthrough discoveries in protein folding and drug development, accelerating scientific progress. Autonomous vehicles navigate complex urban environments with increasing sophistication, while AI systems compose music that challenges our assumptions about creativity and consciousness.

This rapid progression isn't just about technological achievement, it's about fundamental changes in how we live, work, and interact with the world around us. Unlike previous technological revolutions that primarily transformed physical capabilities, AI enhances our cognitive abilities, augmenting human intelligence in unprecedented ways.

Beyond the visible applications lies a vast network of AI systems working behind the scenes. In infrastructure management, smart power grids predict and respond to usage patterns while traffic management systems adapt to real-time conditions. Water distribution networks detect and prevent waste, and communications systems optimize data flow across global networks.

Environmental protection has been enhanced through AI-powered climate modeling systems that predict weather patterns with increasing accuracy. Wildlife conservation efforts benefit from tools that track endangered species across vast territories. Pollution monitoring networks identify sources of contamination, while resource management systems optimize usage to promote sustainability.

In scientific research, AI's impact continues to grow. Astronomical data analysis reveals new celestial phenomena that might otherwise remain hidden in vast datasets. Genetic research accelerates our understanding of human biology, while materials science discovers new compounds with potentially revolutionary applications. The boundaries of quantum computing research advance, promising even more dramatic technological leaps ahead.

The significance of this moment in history cannot be overstated. We are witnessing not just technological evolution, but a fundamental shift in human capability. AI serves as an intelligence amplifier, extending our ability to process vast amounts of information, identify patterns in complex data, make predictions with increasing accuracy, solve problems in novel ways, and create new forms of expression.

This amplification of human capability brings both unprecedented opportunities and significant challenges. As AI systems become more sophisticated, they raise important questions about the future of work and education, the nature of creativity and innovation, the role of human decision-making, the boundaries between human and machine intelligence, and the ethical implications of autonomous systems.

Understanding these developments isn't just about staying informed, it's about preparing for a future where AI literacy becomes as fundamental as digital literacy is today. The decisions we make about AI development and deployment will shape society for generations to come.

The dawn of the AI era brings us to a crucial question: How do we ensure that we not only understand this technology but shape its development in ways that benefit humanity? This journey of understanding isn't just about staying informed, it's about being part of one of the most significant transformations in human history.

With this context in mind, let's examine why understanding AI has become essential for everyone, regardless of their field or background. The implications of AI extend far beyond technology, touching every aspect of our personal and professional lives.

The increasing sophistication and prevalence of AI technologies creates a new imperative for everyone in today's world: AI literacy. This isn't about becoming a technical expert or a programmer. Rather, it represents a fundamental understanding needed to navigate, evaluate, and participate in an AI-enhanced world. Just as reading and writing became essential skills in the age of print, and digital literacy became crucial in the age of computers, AI literacy now emerges as a critical competency for the 21st century.

At its core, this literacy empowers us to maintain autonomy in our decision-making. When AI systems increasingly influence or mediate our choices, understanding their basic principles becomes crucial for maintaining control over our lives and decisions. Without this foundational knowledge, we risk either overestimating AI's capabilities, leading to misplaced trust, or underestimating its potential, missing valuable opportunities. More importantly, we might fail to recognize when and how AI influences our decisions, surrendering our agency without even realizing it.

The professional landscape particularly highlights the necessity of AI understanding. Every profession is evolving with AI, not through wholesale replacement of human workers, but through subtle and significant transformation of how work is done. Lawyers who understand AI can better leverage tools for case research and document analysis. Healthcare professionals who grasp AI's capabilities can better integrate diagnostic support tools into their practice.

Educators who comprehend AI's potential can better prepare students for an AI-enhanced future.

This transformation extends beyond individual professions to entire industries. Business leaders must understand AI sufficiently to make strategic decisions about its implementation. Policy makers need to grasp AI's implications to create effective regulations. Even artists and writers benefit from understanding how AI tools might enhance rather than threaten their creative processes.

The societal impact of AI makes this understanding even more crucial. As AI systems increasingly influence public discourse, shape social interactions, and drive economic changes, informed citizenship requires a basic grasp of AI principles. Without this knowledge, participating meaningfully in crucial public debates about AI regulation, privacy rights, and ethical deployment becomes impossible. How can we contribute to discussions about facial recognition in public spaces, algorithmic decision-making in criminal justice, or AI bias in hiring practices without understanding the fundamental capabilities and limitations of these technologies?

Moreover, this understanding becomes essential for future preparedness. The pace of AI advancement shows no signs of slowing. Those who grasp AI's basic principles will be better positioned to anticipate changes, identify opportunities, and adapt to new developments. Parents and educators need this knowledge to guide younger generations. Business professionals need it to spot emerging trends and opportunities. Citizens need it to participate in shaping policies that will govern AI's development and deployment.

The economic implications amplify this urgency. As AI reshapes markets and transforms business models, understanding its fundamentals becomes crucial for economic participation. Whether evaluating investment opportunities, making career decisions, or planning for retirement, some grasp of AI's potential impact on various sectors becomes essential. This understanding helps distinguish between genuine innovations and mere hype, between transformative technologies and passing fads.

Perhaps most importantly, AI literacy enables us to maintain our role in shaping the future. As AI systems become more sophisticated, the decisions we make about their development and deployment will have far-reaching consequences. These decisions should not be left solely to technical experts. They require input from diverse perspectives, informed by an understanding of both the technology's potential and its limitations.

This understanding serves as a foundation for ethical consideration and critical evaluation of AI developments. It enables us to ask the right questions about AI systems: What biases might they contain? How was their training data collected? What oversight exists for their decisions? Without this baseline knowledge, we risk becoming passive recipients of AI technology rather than active participants in determining its role in our society.

The importance of understanding AI thus extends far beyond mere technological awareness. It becomes a fundamental component of informed decision-making in personal, professional, and civic life. This understanding empowers us to maintain agency in a world where AI increasingly influences decision-making at all levels, from individual choices to societal policies.

As we move forward to explore the core principles and technologies of AI, remember that this knowledge forms the basis for informed participation in the AI era. Understanding these fundamentals will enable you to engage meaningfully with AI developments and contribute to discussions that will shape our collective future.

Building on our understanding of why AI literacy matters, we must now establish a foundational framework for understanding what artificial intelligence actually is. This understanding begins not with complex technical details, which we'll explore in later chapters, but with core principles that define AI's nature and capabilities.

At its most fundamental level, artificial intelligence represents systems that can perform tasks typically associated with human intelligence. Yet this simple definition belies a complex reality. Intelligence itself proves challenging to define, and artificial intelligence even more so. The field encompasses a broad spectrum of capabilities, from narrow, specialized systems to the theoretical possibility of general artificial intelligence.

The contemporary AI landscape primarily consists of narrow or specialized AI systems. These are technologies designed to excel at specific tasks or within defined domains. They might surpass human capabilities in their particular areas, like calculating complex mathematical equations or analyzing vast datasets, while lacking the versatility and adaptability that characterizes human intelligence. This distinction becomes crucial for understanding both the current capabilities and limitations of AI systems.

Consider how this specialization manifests in practice. When we say an AI system is "intelligent," we mean it demonstrates proficiency in its designated task, whether that's recognizing speech, translating languages, or identifying patterns in data. This intelligence differs fundamentally from human intelligence, which naturally generalizes across domains and adapts to new situations. Understanding this distinction helps clarify both the remarkable achievements and inherent limitations of current AI systems.

The concept of artificial general intelligence (AGI) represents a different frontier entirely. AGI refers to hypothetical systems that would match or exceed human-level intelligence across all domains. While this remains in the realm of theoretical possibility rather than current reality, understanding the distinction between narrow AI and AGI provides crucial context for evaluating claims about AI capabilities and potential.

Beyond these categories lies the concept of artificial

superintelligence (ASI), theoretical systems that would significantly surpass human cognitive capabilities. While this concept often captures public imagination and fuels both excitement and concern about AI's future, maintaining focus on current realities while understanding these potential futures helps ground our exploration of AI technologies.

Learning represents another fundamental principle of modern AI systems. Unlike traditional computer programs that follow fixed rules, many AI systems improve their performance through exposure to data and experience. This capability for learning, whether supervised by human input, unsupervised through pattern recognition, or reinforced through trial and error, marks a crucial distinction between AI and conventional software.

The relationship between AI systems and data deserves particular attention. Data serves as both the foundation for AI learning and the context for AI decision-making. Understanding this relationship helps explain both the remarkable capabilities of modern AI systems and their inherent constraints. An AI system can only be as good as the data it learns from, a principle that becomes increasingly important as these systems take on more significant roles in our lives.

Pattern recognition emerges as another core principle underlying many AI capabilities. Whether processing visual information, analyzing text, or making predictions about complex systems, AI's ability to identify patterns in data drives many of its most impressive applications. This fundamental capability explains how AI systems can perform tasks ranging from medical diagnosis to financial forecasting, while also helping us understand their limitations when confronted with scenarios that deviate from recognized patterns.

The concept of optimization also plays a central role in AI systems. Many AI applications work by gradually improving their performance toward specific goals. Understanding this process helps explain both how AI systems improve over time and why they sometimes produce unexpected or unintended results when their optimization goals don't perfectly align with human intentions.

These foundational concepts, specialization, learning, pattern recognition, and optimization, provide a framework for understanding more specific AI technologies and applications that we'll explore throughout this book. They help explain both what current AI systems can achieve and what remains beyond their capabilities.

As we conclude this overview of core principles, we can begin to see how understanding these fundamentals provides a foundation for evaluating AI technologies and their potential impacts. This knowledge framework will prove essential as we explore more specific aspects of AI technology in subsequent chapters.

Let us now turn our attention to examining how these principles manifest in today's AI landscape, where theory meets practical application in ways that continue to reshape our world.

The principles we've explored manifest in today's world through an intricate ecosystem of AI technologies, applications, and innovations. While later chapters will examine specific areas in detail, understanding the broader landscape helps contextualize our journey into AI fundamentals.

Today's AI landscape resembles a vast metropolis, with distinct districts representing different approaches to artificial intelligence. In one area, we find systems focused on perception, technologies that help machines understand the world through sight, sound, and other sensory inputs. In another, we discover systems specialized in processing and generating human language. Yet another district houses AI focused on strategic decision-making and optimization.

What makes this landscape particularly fascinating is how these different approaches increasingly intersect and combine. Modern AI solutions rarely exist in isolation. Instead, they form complex systems that combine multiple capabilities, much like a city's neighborhoods blend into one another, creating unique characteristics at their intersections.

The evolution of this landscape continues at an unprecedented pace, driven by three main factors. First, advances in computational power have enabled more sophisticated AI systems to operate at practical speeds. Second, the explosion of available data provides the raw material these systems need to learn and improve. Third, breakthroughs in AI algorithms and architectures have opened new possibilities for what these systems can achieve.

Understanding this landscape requires recognizing its dynamic nature. Unlike traditional technology implementations, many AI systems continue to evolve after deployment, learning from new data and adapting to changing conditions. This characteristic creates both opportunities and challenges, as systems can improve over time but may also develop in unexpected ways.

The relationship between research and practical application in today's AI landscape proves particularly noteworthy. The gap between theoretical breakthroughs and practical implementations has narrowed dramatically. Ideas that emerge from research laboratories can now find their way into practical applications with remarkable speed, creating a feedback loop that accelerates both scientific understanding and practical innovation.

This rapid evolution has implications for how we approach AI literacy. Rather than focusing on specific technologies that may quickly become outdated, understanding the underlying patterns of AI development and implementation provides more lasting value. These patterns help us recognize both the opportunities and limitations that emerge as new AI capabilities develop.

The economic dimensions of today's AI landscape also merit attention. Investment in AI development has created a complex marketplace where established technology companies, innovative startups, and research institutions all play crucial roles. This diversity of participants helps drive innovation while also raising important questions about access to AI capabilities and the concentration of AI development power.

Perhaps most significantly, today's AI landscape reflects an increasing focus on responsible development and ethical considerations. The recognition that AI systems can perpetuate or amplify existing biases, along with growing awareness of privacy implications and other potential negative impacts, has led to greater emphasis on developing AI systems that are not just powerful, but also trustworthy and beneficial to society.

This broader perspective on the AI landscape helps frame our exploration of specific technologies and applications in subsequent chapters. It reminds us that understanding AI involves more than grasping technical concepts, it requires appreciating the complex interplay of technological capabilities, practical applications, and societal implications.

As we prepare to examine your specific journey through this book, this overview of the AI landscape provides context for the learning path ahead. It helps explain why certain topics deserve particular attention and how different aspects of AI knowledge fit together to form a comprehensive understanding.

Let us now turn our attention to mapping out your journey through this book, understanding how each chapter will build upon this foundation to develop your AI literacy.

Having established the fundamentals of AI and surveyed today's landscape, let us map out the journey ahead. This book is designed to build your understanding progressively, each chapter building upon the foundations laid by those before it. Think of it as an expedition through the territory of artificial intelligence, where each stage reveals new insights while reinforcing previous understanding.

We begin our journey by traveling back in time. The

evolution of artificial intelligence from its earliest conceptual roots to today's sophisticated systems tells a fascinating story of human ingenuity, technological breakthrough, and occasional setbacks. Understanding this history provides more than interesting context, it reveals patterns of development that continue to shape AI's evolution. Through this historical lens, we'll gain insight into why AI has developed along certain paths and what that might tell us about its future direction.

From these historical foundations, we move into deeper territory, exploring the essential concepts that drive modern AI. We'll demystify terms and technologies that often appear in headlines but are rarely explained clearly. This exploration isn't about technical mastery, it's about understanding the fundamental principles that make artificial intelligence possible. We'll clear away the fog of jargon and hyperbole to reveal the actual mechanisms that enable AI systems to perform their remarkable feats.

Our journey then takes us into the realm of AI types and capabilities. The distinctions between narrow AI, general AI, and superintelligence become crucial for understanding both current realities and future possibilities. This knowledge proves essential for evaluating claims about AI capabilities and making informed decisions about AI applications.

As we venture further, we'll explore the core technologies that power today's AI revolution. Machine learning, neural networks, and natural language processing emerge not as intimidating technical concepts but as understandable approaches to solving complex problems. We'll examine how these technologies work together, creating systems greater than the sum of their parts.

The practical mechanics of AI form another crucial territory in our exploration. Understanding how AI systems learn from data, how they make decisions, and how they improve over time provides essential insight into both their capabilities and limitations. This knowledge proves particularly valuable when evaluating AI solutions or

25

considering their implementation.

Our journey then moves into the practical world, examining how AI technologies translate into real-world applications. Rather than focusing on technical specifications, we'll explore how these technologies actually solve problems and create value across different domains. This practical perspective helps bridge the gap between theoretical understanding and actual implementation.

We'll then explore the crucial limitations and constraints that shape AI system operation. Understanding these boundaries, from technical constraints to operational challenges, proves essential for realistic implementation and effective use of AI technology. This examination of limitations helps set appropriate expectations while ensuring responsible system deployment.

As our expedition continues, we'll navigate the crucial territory of ethical considerations. The development and deployment of AI technologies raise important questions about privacy, bias, and the relationship between human and machine decision-making. Understanding these challenges becomes essential for responsible engagement with AI technology.

The issue of AI bias receives special attention in our journey, as it represents one of the most significant challenges in current AI development. We'll explore how bias enters AI systems and, more importantly, how it can be recognized and addressed. This knowledge proves crucial for ensuring AI systems serve all of society equitably.

Our path then leads us through the complex landscape of privacy considerations in the AI era. As AI systems process increasing amounts of personal data, understanding the implications for privacy becomes essential. We'll explore how to balance the benefits of AI with the fundamental right to privacy.

The principles and practices of responsible AI development form another crucial territory in our journey.

We'll examine how AI can be developed and deployed in ways that benefit society while minimizing potential negative impacts. This knowledge becomes increasingly important as AI systems take on more significant roles in our lives.

As we near the end of our journey, we'll explore AI's potential for addressing global challenges. Understanding how AI can contribute to solving major societal problems helps place this technology in a broader context of human progress and development.

Finally, we'll look toward the horizon, examining trends and developments that may shape AI's future evolution. This forward-looking perspective helps prepare you for continued engagement with AI as it develops.

Throughout this journey, our focus remains on building practical understanding rather than technical expertise. Each chapter contributes to a comprehensive framework for understanding AI, making informed decisions about its use, and participating in discussions about its development.

Throughout this book, you'll notice certain fundamental AI concepts appear multiple times, examined from different angles and in varying contexts. This intentional approach serves several purposes. Key concepts like machine learning, neural networks, or data processing first appear in basic definition, then return as we explore their development, examine their mechanics, and see their practical applications. This layered revisiting of core concepts helps reinforce understanding while revealing how these elements work both independently and in combination.

For instance, when we first introduce machine learning, we focus on its basic definition. Later, we examine how it develops and functions. Still later, we see how it combines with other AI elements and works in real-world applications. This deliberate repetition strengthens the learning process and demonstrates the interconnected nature of AI systems. As you encounter familiar concepts in new contexts, you'll develop deeper understanding of their significance and relationships within the broader AI landscape. Let us now examine the specific path forward that will guide us through this exploration.

The journey we've outlined requires more than just following a map, it needs a thoughtful approach to learning and understanding. This section addresses how we'll navigate the complexities of artificial intelligence together, building knowledge systematically while maintaining practical relevance throughout our exploration.

Our approach emphasizes understanding over memorization. Rather than simply accumulating facts about AI, we'll develop a framework for thinking about these technologies and their implications. This framework will serve you well beyond the pages of this book, providing a foundation for evaluating new AI developments as they emerge.

Throughout our journey, we'll maintain a balance between technical understanding and practical application. While we'll explore the underlying concepts that make AI possible, we'll consistently connect these ideas to real-world contexts. This connection between theory and practice helps make abstract concepts concrete and memorable.

Critical thinking serves as our constant companion on this journey. Each topic we explore will include not just explanation but also examination, considering implications, questioning assumptions, and evaluating potential impacts. This analytical approach helps develop not just knowledge about AI, but the ability to evaluate new developments as they arise.

As artificial intelligence continues to evolve, the ability to adapt and learn becomes crucial. Our approach therefore emphasizes understanding fundamental principles that remain relevant even as specific technologies change. Think of these principles as anchors, providing stability amid rapid technological evolution while allowing flexibility in how they're applied.

AI BASICS: THE FUNDAMENTALS

The complexity of AI might seem daunting, but our path forward breaks this complexity into manageable pieces. Each chapter builds upon previous understanding, creating a progressive journey that develops knowledge systematically. This building-block approach allows us to tackle sophisticated concepts by first establishing solid foundations.

Our exploration will consistently connect individual topics to the broader context of AI development and implementation. Understanding how different aspects of AI relate to each other helps create a more complete and useful picture of this technology. This interconnected understanding proves particularly valuable when evaluating AI solutions or considering their implementation.

As we progress, we'll develop both knowledge and analytical skills. Understanding AI requires not just knowing what these technologies can do, but also being able to evaluate their appropriate use. This combination of knowledge and critical thinking ability provides the foundation for informed decision-making about AI technologies.

The path forward also involves developing a vocabulary for discussing AI effectively. Rather than getting lost in technical jargon, we'll focus on understanding and articulating key concepts clearly. This ability to communicate about AI proves invaluable whether you're evaluating AI solutions, implementing AI technologies, or participating in discussions about AI's role in society.

Perhaps most importantly, our path maintains a focus on practical relevance. While we'll explore fascinating theoretical concepts, we'll consistently return to how this knowledge applies in real-world contexts. This practical focus helps ensure that the understanding you develop translates into useful capabilities.

The journey ahead promises to be both challenging and rewarding. As artificial intelligence continues to reshape our world, the understanding you develop will prove increasingly valuable. Let us begin our detailed exploration with the foundation of all technological progress: understanding where we've been and how we've arrived at our current moment.

As we conclude this introduction to AI basics, we stand at the beginning of a fascinating journey into one of the most transformative technologies of our time. We've established that artificial intelligence isn't just a collection of technologies, it represents a fundamental shift in how we process information, solve problems, and interact with the world around us.

Our exploration has revealed the multifaceted nature of AI's impact, from its seamless integration into daily life to its profound implications for society's future. We've seen why understanding AI matters now more than ever, not just for specialists but for everyone participating in our increasingly AI-enhanced world. The core principles and technologies we've touched upon provide a foundation for the deeper understanding we'll develop throughout this book.

The current AI landscape, as we've discovered, presents both extraordinary opportunities and significant challenges. Yet understanding this landscape requires more than just knowing what AI can do, it demands appreciation for how these technologies develop, deploy, and evolve. This understanding becomes particularly crucial as AI continues to expand its influence across every sector of society.

The path we've outlined through this book reflects the systematic way we'll build this understanding. Each chapter ahead will illuminate different aspects of AI, from its historical evolution to its future possibilities. This journey will develop not just your knowledge of AI, but your ability to think critically about its development and implementation.

As we move forward into our detailed exploration of AI's evolution in the next chapter, remember that this journey isn't just about learning technology, it's about preparing to participate meaningfully in shaping AI's role in our world. The foundations we've established here will support our investigation of more specific aspects of AI, ensuring that each new concept builds upon solid understanding.

The questions we've raised about AI's nature, impact, and future set the stage for deeper exploration. How did AI evolve from early concepts to today's sophisticated systems? What principles drive its current development? How can we ensure its deployment benefits society as a whole? These questions and more will guide our continued investigation.

Our next chapter begins this detailed exploration by examining the fascinating history of artificial intelligence. Through understanding how AI evolved from its earliest conceptual roots to today's sophisticated systems, we'll gain crucial insight into both its current capabilities and its future potential.

The journey ahead promises to be both enlightening and engaging. Let us turn now to the beginning of this story, where human ingenuity first began to imagine machines that could think.

CHAPTER 2: THE EVOLUTION OF AI

The story of artificial intelligence begins long before the first computer was built, rooted in humanity's age-old fascination with the possibility of creating machines that could think. This ambition, which now drives one of the most dynamic fields in technology, emerged from a rich tapestry of mathematical theory, philosophical inquiry, and technological innovation.

Understanding these early foundations proves crucial for appreciating how artificial intelligence evolved into the transformative force we explored in Chapter 1. The path from early concepts to modern AI reveals not just technological progress, but the persistent human drive to expand the boundaries of what machines can achieve.

The theoretical groundwork for artificial intelligence began taking concrete form in the early 20th century, as mathematicians and philosophers developed new ways of thinking about computation and reasoning. Boolean logic, developed by George Boole in the mid-19th century, provided a mathematical framework for representing logical thinking, a framework that would later prove essential for computational reasoning. These mathematical foundations, combined with advances in engineering and electronics, set the stage for a revolutionary leap in human thought about machines and intelligence.

The pivotal moment in this early period came in 1936, when a young British mathematician named Alan Turing introduced a concept that would fundamentally change our understanding of computation. His paper "On Computable Numbers" introduced the idea of a universal computing machine, what we now call the Turing Machine. This theoretical device, though never built as Turing envisioned it, established the mathematical foundation for all modern computers and, by extension, artificial intelligence.

Turing's genius lay in recognizing that a machine could manipulate symbols according to rules to compute any calculable function. This insight transcended the limited view of computers as mere calculating devices, suggesting instead that they could potentially simulate any form of logical reasoning. The implications were profound: if thinking could be reduced to mathematical processes, then machines might someday be capable of thought.

In 1950, Turing took this idea further with his seminal paper "Computing Machinery and Intelligence." Here, he directly addressed the question that would come to define the field of AI: "Can machines think?" Rather than getting lost in philosophical debates about the nature of consciousness, Turing proposed a practical test, now known as the Turing Test, to evaluate machine intelligence. The test suggested that if a machine could engage in conversation so convincingly that humans couldn't distinguish it from another human, we would have to consider the possibility that the machine was thinking.

During this same period, another crucial strand of thought was developing through the work of Norbert Wiener. In the 1940s, Wiener established the field of cybernetics, publishing his groundbreaking work "Cybernetics: Or Control and

Communication in the Animal and the Machine" in 1948. Wiener's work examined how systems, both biological and mechanical, process information, make decisions, and correct their behavior through feedback. His ideas about feedback systems and control mechanisms would prove fundamental to later developments in robotics and artificial intelligence.

Wiener's cybernetics provided a crucial bridge between biological and mechanical systems, suggesting that both could be understood through the same principles of information processing and control. This perspective helped establish the intellectual framework necessary for considering how machines might replicate or simulate biological intelligence.

These early foundations, Turing's theoretical framework for computation, his philosophical inquiries into machine intelligence, and Wiener's cybernetic principles, created the intellectual environment from which modern artificial intelligence would emerge. They demonstrated that questions about machine intelligence could be approached scientifically, setting the stage for the practical work that would follow.

As we transition into the 1950s, these theoretical foundations would soon be tested against the practical challenges of creating intelligent machines. The stage was set for a gathering that would formally establish the field of artificial intelligence and launch a new era in human technological achievement.

The 1950s marked the transition from theoretical foundations to practical pursuit of artificial intelligence. While Turing and Wiener had established crucial groundwork, it would take a gathering of brilliant minds to formally launch the field of artificial intelligence as we know it today.

The pivotal moment came in the summer of 1956 at Dartmouth College. John McCarthy, then a young assistant professor of mathematics, organized what would become known as the Dartmouth Conference, an eight-week summit that formally birthed the field of artificial intelligence. McCarthy's vision was boldly ambitious: to explore ways that machines could simulate every aspect of learning and intelligence.

The conference proposal, co-authored by McCarthy, Marvin Minsky, Nathaniel Rochester, and Claude Shannon, outlined an audacious goal: "to proceed on the basis of the conjecture that every aspect of learning or any other feature of intelligence can in principle be so precisely described that a machine can be made to simulate it." This statement, remarkable for its time, encapsulates both the optimism and the fundamental assumption that would drive AI research for decades to come.

The participants themselves represented a remarkable concentration of intellectual talent. John McCarthy brought his expertise in mathematical logic and his belief in the possibility of mechanical reasoning. Marvin Minsky contributed his insights into neural networks and learning systems. Claude Shannon, already famous for developing information theory, provided crucial theoretical frameworks for understanding how machines might process information. Nathaniel Rochester, from IBM, brought practical computing expertise and industry perspective.

The Dartmouth Conference proved groundbreaking in multiple ways. First, it was here that McCarthy coined the term "artificial intelligence," giving the field its enduring name. This naming was more than mere semantics, it represented a clear statement that the goal was to create genuine intelligence in artificial systems, not just to simulate human behavior.

During those eight weeks, the participants engaged in wide-ranging discussions and collaborations that would shape the future of AI research. While not all attendees stayed for the entire period, the conference established key research directions and fostered collaborations that would continue for decades. The participants shared a common optimism about the possibility of creating machines that could think, though they differed in their approaches to achieving this goal.

One of the most significant outcomes emerged shortly

after the conference, when Allen Newell and Herbert A. Simon, who had attended parts of the gathering, developed the Logic Theorist. This program, often considered the first artificial intelligence program, could prove mathematical theorems using symbolic reasoning. Its success in proving theorems from Whitehead and Russell's "Principia Mathematica" demonstrated that machines could indeed perform tasks requiring intelligence.

McCarthy's own contributions extended beyond organizing the conference. In 1958, he developed LISP (List Processing), a programming language specifically designed for AI research. LISP's ability to manipulate symbolic expressions rather than just numbers made it ideal for AI applications, and it would remain the dominant language in AI research for decades.

The conference also established distinct approaches to artificial intelligence that would compete and complement each other in the years ahead. Some participants favored symbolic reasoning, attempting to encode human knowledge and logic directly into computer programs. Others were more interested in neural networks and learning systems that could develop their own problem-solving approaches.

This diversity of approaches reflected a crucial understanding: that intelligence might be achieved through multiple paths, each offering unique insights into the nature of thinking and problem-solving. The conference participants recognized that creating artificial intelligence would require exploring various approaches, from logical reasoning to pattern recognition to learning from experience.

As the conference concluded, its participants dispersed to various institutions, carrying with them the shared vision of artificial intelligence as a distinct field of study. They established AI laboratories at their respective institutions, began training students, and launched research programs that would form the foundation of AI development for years to come.

The Dartmouth Conference marked not just the birth of a new field, but the beginning of a new era in human technological achievement. It set in motion a series of developments that would lead to both remarkable successes and sobering setbacks, as researchers began the practical work of trying to create thinking machines.

Following the historic Dartmouth Conference of 1956, artificial intelligence research expanded along several distinct paths. Each approach represented a different vision of how to create intelligent machines, leading to a period of remarkable innovation and discovery.

John McCarthy, fresh from his role in organizing the Dartmouth Conference, focused on developing tools that could help machines process information more like humans. In 1958, he created LISP (List Processing), a programming language specifically designed for AI research. LISP gave researchers a new way to write programs that could process symbols and ideas, not just numbers, a fundamental requirement for simulating human-like reasoning.

During this same period, another fascinating approach to artificial intelligence emerged from our understanding of the human brain. In 1943, Warren McCulloch and Walter Pitts had proposed the first mathematical model of a neural network, a computing system inspired by the way biological brains process information. This theoretical foundation led to an exciting breakthrough in 1958, when Frank Rosenblatt introduced the Perceptron, the first practical artificial neural network. The Perceptron demonstrated that machines could learn from experience, generating tremendous excitement about this new approach to AI.

Meanwhile, Allen Newell and Herbert A. Simon pursued yet another direction. Their Logic Theorist program, developed shortly after the Dartmouth Conference, became the first program to mimic human problem-solving. It successfully proved mathematical theorems, demonstrating that machines could perform tasks requiring logical reasoning.

Building on this success, they created the General Problem Solver (GPS) in 1957, which could tackle a broader range of puzzles and problems.

The field of natural language processing, teaching computers to understand human language, emerged as another crucial area of research. In 1964, Joseph Weizenbaum at MIT created ELIZA, a program that could engage in written dialogue with humans. While ELIZA simply followed programmed patterns rather than truly understanding language, it demonstrated the possibility of human-computer interaction through natural conversation.

Computer vision also took its first steps during this period. Larry Roberts at MIT showed that computers could analyze simple images and understand three-dimensional space, laying groundwork for future developments in machine perception.

The optimism of this era was captured by Marvin Minsky's 1967 prediction that "within a generation... the problem of creating 'artificial intelligence' will substantially be solved." This confidence reflected the field's early successes and the belief that continued progress was just a matter of time and effort.

However, as researchers attempted more complex tasks, they began to encounter unexpected challenges. Each approach showed promise in specific areas but revealed limitations when tackling broader problems. These challenges would soon lead the field into a period of reassessment, but the fundamental approaches established during this first wave, symbolic reasoning, neural networks, and machine learning, had laid crucial groundwork for future developments.

The boundless optimism of AI's first decade began to encounter serious challenges as the 1960s drew to a close. Each of the promising approaches developed during AI's first wave would face limitations that revealed just how complex the challenge of creating artificial intelligence truly was.

A pivotal moment came in 1969 with the publication of "Perceptrons" by Marvin Minsky and Seymour Papert. Their mathematical analysis revealed fundamental limitations in what Rosenblatt's Perceptron could achieve. The impact of their work was profound and immediate. Research funding for neural network approaches virtually disappeared, effectively pausing this line of research for over a decade.

While neural network research declined, McCarthy's symbolic approach to AI, using rules and logic to represent knowledge, encountered its own challenges. Researchers discovered that giving computers "common sense" understanding proved far more difficult than anticipated. Tasks that humans perform effortlessly, like understanding simple stories or recognizing objects in different situations, revealed themselves to be enormously complex when researchers tried to reduce them to logical rules.

Natural language research faced similar obstacles. While programs like ELIZA had created an illusion of language understanding, creating systems that truly comprehended human communication proved far more challenging than expected. Researchers began to realize that understanding language required not just processing words and grammar, but comprehending the broader context of human experience.

These mounting challenges culminated in 1973 with the publication of the Lighthill Report in the United Kingdom. Sir James Lighthill, commissioned by the British Science Research Council, delivered a comprehensive critique of artificial intelligence research. His report questioned not just the field's progress but its fundamental premises, arguing that AI had failed to achieve its grand objectives.

The Lighthill Report's impact extended far beyond Britain's borders. Government agencies and corporations worldwide began questioning their investments in AI research. Funding cuts followed, leading to what became known as the first "AI Winter", a period of reduced funding, diminished expectations, and limited research progress.

This winter, however, forced the field to mature in important ways. Rather than pursuing grandiose visions of general artificial intelligence, researchers began focusing on more specialized applications that could solve specific practical problems. This shift in perspective would eventually lead to one of AI's first practical successes: expert systems.

The lesson of this period was clear: creating artificial intelligence would require more than just clever programming or faster computers. It would demand a deeper understanding of intelligence itself, along with new approaches that could overcome the limitations of early methods.

As artificial intelligence emerged from its first winter, a new direction offered hope for the field. Rather than trying to create general-purpose thinking machines, researchers began focusing on capturing specific types of human expertise in narrow domains. This more focused approach would lead to one of AI's first practical successes.

At Stanford University, Edward Feigenbaum and Joshua Lederberg pioneered this new direction with DENDRAL, an expert system designed to help chemists identify molecular structures. DENDRAL represented a significant shift in AI development, instead of trying to reason from basic principles, it captured the specific knowledge and problem-solving strategies of expert chemists. The system's success demonstrated that AI could solve real-world problems when focused on well-defined areas of expertise.

Building on this approach, a team at Stanford developed an even more influential system in the early 1970s. MYCIN, created by Edward Shortliffe under the guidance of Bruce Buchanan, Stanley N. Cohen, and Joshua Lederberg, was designed to help doctors diagnose blood infections and recommend appropriate antibiotics. The system's performance matched or sometimes exceeded that of experienced physicians, proving that computers could effectively apply expert knowledge in complex medical situations.

The success of DENDRAL and MYCIN sparked widespread interest in expert systems. Companies began developing specialized systems for various industries, from manufacturing to finance. For the first time, artificial intelligence had found its way out of research laboratories and into practical business applications.

This era marked AI's first significant commercial success. Organizations worldwide began investing in expert systems, seeing their potential to capture and apply specialized knowledge. The technology had found its first viable business model, leading to the creation of specialized AI companies and departments within larger corporations.

However, the development of expert systems revealed new challenges. Capturing expert knowledge proved more complex than initially anticipated. Experts often found it difficult to explain exactly how they made their decisions, and their knowledge frequently relied on intuitions that proved hard to translate into computer instructions.

Moreover, these systems showed limitations that would ultimately lead to disillusionment. They performed well within their specialized domains but couldn't adapt to new situations or handle problems that required common sense reasoning. When confronted with situations slightly outside their programmed expertise, they often failed in ways that humans would find obvious.

Despite these limitations, the expert systems era made several lasting contributions to AI development. It demonstrated that artificial intelligence could solve real-world problems and provide practical value when focused on specific domains. Perhaps most importantly, it showed the value of narrowing AI's focus to well-defined problems rather than trying to create general intelligence immediately.

As the 1980s progressed, the limitations of expert systems would become increasingly apparent. However, this period coincided with renewed interest in neural networks, driven by new theoretical insights and improving computer technology. The field of AI was about to undergo another fundamental shift in approach, one that would eventually lead to many of today's most significant achievements.

After nearly two decades of dormancy following Minsky and Papert's critique, neural networks experienced a remarkable revival in the 1980s. This renaissance emerged from new theoretical insights that overcame many of the limitations identified in the 1969 "Perceptrons" book.

A key breakthrough came through the work of Geoffrey Hinton and his colleagues in the mid-1980s. Their research demonstrated that neural networks could learn complex patterns more effectively than previously thought possible. This discovery, combined with increasing computer power, sparked renewed interest in this approach to artificial intelligence.

The revival of neural networks marked a fundamental shift in how researchers approached AI development. Rather than programming explicit rules and knowledge into computers, as expert systems had done, these systems could learn patterns from examples, more closely resembling how humans learn from experience.

Throughout the late 1980s and early 1990s, neural networks demonstrated success in various practical applications, particularly in pattern recognition tasks. This progress helped restore confidence in neural network research, which had been largely abandoned during the previous two decades.

While neural networks were gaining renewed attention, another landmark in AI development captured the world's imagination. In 1997, IBM's Deep Blue chess computer achieved what many had thought impossible: it defeated world champion Garry Kasparov in a six-game match under standard chess tournament conditions.

The match drew global attention and marked a significant milestone in artificial intelligence. For the first time, a computer had defeated a reigning world champion in a game long considered a testament to human intellectual capability. While chess mastery represented only a narrow slice of human intelligence, Deep Blue's victory demonstrated that computers could outperform humans in tasks requiring sophisticated strategic thinking.

Deep Blue's success, combined with the renewed progress in neural networks, helped restore public and academic interest in artificial intelligence. These achievements showed that different approaches to AI could succeed when focused on specific types of problems.

As the 1990s drew to a close, the field of artificial intelligence had been transformed. The success of both neural networks and specialized systems like Deep Blue demonstrated AI's growing capabilities while pointing toward future developments. The stage was set for even more dramatic advances in the decades to come.

The arrival of the 2000s marked the beginning of a new era in artificial intelligence, one that would see breakthroughs occurring at an unprecedented pace. The stage was set for what would become known as the deep learning revolution, transforming AI from a specialized research field into a technology that touches nearly every aspect of modern life.

A pivotal moment came in 2012 when Geoffrey Hinton and his team at the University of Toronto achieved record-breaking results in image recognition. Their breakthrough demonstrated the remarkable potential of deep learning, igniting a new wave of AI research and development that continues to this day.

The field reached another milestone in 2016 when DeepMind's AlphaGo defeated world champion Lee Sedol at the game of Go. This achievement resonated even more deeply than Deep Blue's chess victory two decades earlier. Go's complexity had led many to believe it would remain beyond the reach of artificial intelligence for decades to come. AlphaGo's victory demonstrated just how far AI capabilities had advanced.

The year 2015 saw the founding of OpenAI, established with the mission of ensuring that artificial general intelligence

(AGI) benefits all of humanity. OpenAI would go on to make significant contributions to the field, particularly in natural language processing. Their development of increasingly sophisticated language models, culminating in GPT-3's release in 2020, demonstrated AI's growing ability to understand and generate human-like text.

These advances were made possible by several converging factors: exponential increases in computing power, the availability of vast amounts of digital data for training AI systems, and fundamental improvements in AI algorithms. Together, these elements enabled artificial intelligence to tackle increasingly complex challenges.

The impact of these developments extended far beyond research laboratories. AI technologies began appearing in everyday life through applications like voice assistants, recommendation systems, and automated translation services. In specialized fields like healthcare, AI systems started assisting with medical diagnosis and drug discovery. In transportation, AI became crucial to the development of autonomous vehicle technologies.

This period demonstrates how far artificial intelligence has come from its origins at the Dartmouth Conference. What began as a small group of researchers exploring the possibility of machine intelligence has grown into a global enterprise that is reshaping how we live and work.

Yet even as we marvel at these achievements, it's worth remembering that they build upon the foundations laid by early pioneers. The symbolic reasoning approaches of McCarthy, the neural network insights of Rosenblatt, the expert systems of Feigenbaum, each contributed crucial insights that inform today's developments.

As artificial intelligence continues to evolve, the pace of innovation shows no signs of slowing. Each breakthrough opens new possibilities while raising important questions about how these technologies will shape our future. Understanding this history helps us appreciate both how far we've come and the exciting developments that lie ahead.

As we conclude our journey through AI's evolution, certain patterns emerge that help us understand not just where artificial intelligence has been, but where it might be heading. From the early optimism of the Dartmouth Conference to today's rapid developments, the field has moved through distinct cycles of breakthrough, challenge, and renewal.

Each era brought its own vision of how to create intelligent machines. McCarthy and his colleagues pursued symbolic reasoning, believing that human intelligence could be reduced to logical rules. Rosenblatt's Perceptron suggested that machines might learn from experience, much as humans do. Expert systems demonstrated the value of capturing specialized knowledge. Today's deep learning approaches combine aspects of these earlier visions while pushing into new territory.

The field's development has not followed a straight line. Periods of rapid progress have alternated with times of reassessment. The AI winters, while challenging, served as crucial periods of maturation. Each setback forced researchers to reevaluate their assumptions and approaches, ultimately leading to stronger foundations for future progress.

This historical perspective reveals an important truth: significant breakthroughs often come not just from new technologies, but from new ways of thinking about old problems. The neural network renaissance of the 1980s succeeded precisely because researchers found fresh approaches to challenges that had seemed insurmountable a decade earlier.

Understanding this history proves essential as we prepare to explore artificial intelligence in greater depth. Each technology we'll examine in upcoming chapters, from machine learning to natural language processing, has roots in the historical developments we've traced. The challenges and successes of the past continue to inform how we approach AI development today.

AI BASICS: THE FUNDAMENTALS

The questions raised by AI's pioneers remain relevant: How can machines learn from experience? How do we represent knowledge in computational forms? How do we bridge the gap between narrow specialized capabilities and more general intelligence? While our technological capabilities have advanced tremendously, these fundamental questions continue to guide research and development.

As we move forward in this book to examine specific AI technologies and applications, this historical context will help us better understand both their capabilities and limitations. The path from Turing's universal machine to today's AI systems has been marked by both remarkable achievements and humbling challenges. Each development we'll explore builds upon this rich history of innovation and discovery.

In our next chapter, we'll begin to demystify the core concepts of artificial intelligence, building upon the historical foundation we've established. Understanding where AI came from helps us better appreciate where it is going, and how we can participate in shaping its future development.

GIL OREN

CHAPTER 3: DEMYSTIFYING AI

Having traced artificial intelligence from its earliest concepts through decades of development, we now stand in a moment where AI touches nearly every aspect of modern life. Our historical journey has shown us how we arrived here; now it's time to understand what AI actually is and how it works at its most fundamental level.

Think of our exploration so far as similar to learning about the automobile. We began with the history, from the first dreams of self-powered vehicles through the development of the internal combustion engine to modern cars. Now, we need to understand the basic principles that make cars work, not to become mechanics, but to be informed drivers and users of the technology.

The same holds true for artificial intelligence. While AI researchers and developers need deep technical knowledge, every informed citizen today needs a clear understanding of AI's basic principles. This understanding helps us navigate an AI-enhanced world, make informed decisions about AI tools and applications, and participate in crucial discussions about

AI's role in society.

Our goal in this chapter is simple but powerful: to demystify artificial intelligence. We'll break down complex concepts into understandable ideas, using familiar examples from daily life. Rather than delving into technical details, which we'll explore in later chapters, we'll focus on building a solid conceptual foundation.

We'll explore three fundamental building blocks that form the core of modern AI systems: machine learning, neural networks, and natural language processing. Think of these as the engine, transmission, and steering wheel of AI, each playing a crucial role in making these systems work. Understanding these basics helps clarify both the capabilities and limitations of current AI technology.

Just as importantly, we'll look at how these components work together, supported by data and algorithms, to create the AI systems we encounter every day. From smartphones to smart homes, from online shopping to digital entertainment, we'll see how these basic principles manifest in practical applications.

This understanding becomes particularly valuable as AI continues to evolve. The historical perspective we gained in Chapter 2 showed us how AI has developed through waves of innovation and refinement. As we move forward, grasping these fundamental concepts will help us better understand each new development and its potential impact.

Let's begin our exploration of these basics, building a framework for understanding that will serve us throughout our journey into artificial intelligence.

At its heart, artificial intelligence is the creation of computer systems that can perform tasks typically requiring human intelligence. This simple definition opens the door to understanding both the promise and complexity of AI. While human intelligence encompasses countless capabilities, from recognizing faces to solving complex problems, AI approaches these tasks differently than humans do.

AI BASICS: THE FUNDAMENTALS

Consider how you recognize a friend's face in a photograph. You do this instantly, without conscious thought about specific features or mathematical calculations. An AI system, however, analyzes patterns of pixels, identifying key features and comparing them against known patterns. While the end result might be the same, correctly identifying a face, the process differs fundamentally from human recognition.

This difference highlights an important truth about artificial intelligence: it doesn't replicate human thought processes. Instead, it achieves similar results through different means. When we say a machine is "intelligent," we mean it can produce results that would require intelligence if performed by humans, not that it thinks the way humans do.

We experience this form of machine intelligence daily, often without realizing it. When your email program filters spam, it's using AI to analyze messages and make decisions. When your phone's camera automatically adjusts to capture the best possible photo, it's using AI to analyze the scene and optimize settings. When your music streaming service recommends songs you might like, it's using AI to understand patterns in your listening history.

These everyday examples reveal another important aspect of artificial intelligence: it excels at specific, well-defined tasks. Your email program might be excellent at filtering spam, but it can't help you compose a heartfelt message to a friend. Your camera can optimize technical settings but can't tell you which moments are worth capturing. Your music service can recommend songs but can't create new music (though other AI systems are beginning to do this).

Understanding this task-specific nature of current AI helps us appreciate both its capabilities and limitations. While AI can process vast amounts of data and recognize complex patterns far faster than humans, it lacks the general intelligence and adaptability that humans possess naturally. It can be trained to excel at specific tasks but doesn't have the broad understanding and flexibility that characterize human intelligence.

This brings us to another crucial point: artificial intelligence, as we experience it today, learns from data. Unlike traditional computer programs that follow fixed rules, AI systems can improve their performance through exposure to more information. This ability to learn, to get better at tasks through experience, represents one of the most significant advances in computing technology.

As we move forward to explore the building blocks of AI systems, keep in mind this fundamental understanding: artificial intelligence is about creating systems that can perform intelligent tasks, even though they may approach these tasks very differently than humans do. This perspective helps us appreciate both the remarkable capabilities of current AI systems and the challenges that lie ahead in their development.

Just as a house needs a foundation, walls, and a roof, modern artificial intelligence systems are built from three essential components. Each plays a crucial role in creating the AI applications we use every day. Understanding these building blocks, machine learning, neural networks, and natural language processing, helps us grasp how AI systems work without getting lost in technical details.

Machine learning represents perhaps the most fundamental shift in how computers operate. Traditional computer programs follow strict rules set by programmers, if this happens, do that. Machine learning takes a different approach: instead of following fixed rules, these systems learn from experience.

Think about how you might teach a child to recognize dogs. You wouldn't give them a list of precise measurements or mathematical formulas. Instead, you would show them many examples of dogs until they learned to recognize them on their own. Machine learning works similarly. By examining many examples, these systems learn to recognize patterns and make decisions.

We experience the results of machine learning in countless

ways throughout our daily lives. When your video streaming service suggests shows you might enjoy, it's learning from your viewing history and the preferences of viewers with similar tastes. Your phone's keyboard predicts your next word by learning from your writing patterns and common language usage. Credit card companies protect your accounts by learning to recognize the difference between your normal purchasing patterns and suspicious activities that might indicate fraud.

If machine learning represents how AI systems learn, neural networks represent their underlying structure. Inspired by the human brain's billions of interconnected neurons, neural networks are systems designed to recognize patterns in much the same way our brains do.

Consider how you recognize a song. Whether it's played on a piano, guitar, or sung a cappella, you can identify it because your brain recognizes the underlying pattern of the melody. Neural networks, particularly deep learning systems, work similarly. They excel at finding patterns in complex information, whether that's identifying objects in images, recognizing speech, or understanding language patterns.

These pattern recognition capabilities have become an integral part of our daily technology interactions. Each time we unlock our phones with facial recognition, the system uses neural networks to analyze the image and confirm our identity. When we speak to virtual assistants, neural networks help convert our speech into text and understand our requests. Translation apps use these systems to recognize and convert patterns between different languages, making communication across language barriers increasingly natural and effective.

The third building block, natural language processing (NLP), focuses on bridging the gap between human communication and computer understanding. It's what allows machines to understand, interpret, and respond to human language in useful ways.

Think about how complex human language is. We use

idioms, metaphors, and context. We understand nuance and implied meaning. While current NLP systems don't grasp language exactly as humans do, they can understand enough to be remarkably useful. When you interact with a virtual assistant or use an email system that automatically categorizes messages, you're experiencing the power of natural language processing.

The complexity of this task becomes clear when we consider what happens during a simple interaction with a smartphone's assistant. When you ask about the weather, multiple layers of processing occur seamlessly. The system converts your speech to text, analyzes the meaning of your words, understands that you're making a weather inquiry, determines your location, fetches relevant weather data, formulates an appropriate response, and converts that response back into speech. While this might seem straightforward to us, it represents a remarkable achievement in machine understanding of human communication.

These three building blocks, machine learning, neural networks, and natural language processing, work together in modern AI systems. Machine learning provides the ability to improve through experience, neural networks offer powerful pattern recognition, and NLP enables natural communication between humans and machines.

Understanding these components helps us appreciate both the capabilities and limitations of current AI systems. While each component is powerful, they work best when focused on specific, well-defined tasks. As we'll explore in later chapters, the technical details of how these components work reveal both their remarkable capabilities and their current constraints.

If the three building blocks we just explored represent the structure of AI systems, then data and algorithms form the foundation upon which everything else rests. Understanding their basic role helps complete our picture of how artificial intelligence works.

Data is the raw material from which AI systems learn and operate. Just as humans learn from experience, AI systems learn from data. But what exactly do we mean by data? In the context of AI, data can be almost anything, images, text, numbers, measurements, recordings, or any other type of information that can be processed by computers.

Think about how a child learns to read. They need to see many examples of letters and words, hear them pronounced, and practice recognizing them in different contexts. Similarly, an AI system learning to recognize text needs examples, thousands or even millions of them. The more quality examples it receives, the better it becomes at its task.

We contribute to this learning process every day, often without realizing it. When you tag friends in photos, you're helping create training data for facial recognition systems. When you click on recommended products, you're providing data about consumer preferences. When you use a navigation app, you're contributing data about traffic patterns.

The quality and quantity of data directly impact an AI system's performance. Just as a student can't learn effectively from incorrect information, AI systems need accurate, relevant data to perform well. This helps explain why AI has advanced so rapidly in recent years, our digital world generates enormous amounts of data that these systems can learn from.

If data is the raw material, then algorithms are the instructions for processing that material. An algorithm is simply a set of steps for solving a problem or completing a task. While this might sound complex, we use algorithms in everyday life. A cooking recipe is an algorithm, it provides steps to transform ingredients (data) into a finished dish.

In AI systems, algorithms determine how the system learns from data and makes decisions. They're the instructions that guide how neural networks process information, how machine learning systems improve their performance, and how natural language processing interprets human communication.

Think of a music recommendation system. The data includes your listening history, other users' preferences, and information about songs. The algorithms are the instructions for analyzing this data to find patterns and make suggestions. While the specific instructions might be complex, the basic idea is straightforward: analyze patterns in the data to make informed predictions.

Data and algorithms work hand in hand in AI systems. The best algorithm won't perform well without good data to work with, and the best data won't be useful without effective algorithms to process it. This relationship helps explain both the capabilities and limitations of current AI systems.

We can see this partnership at work in the voice assistant on your smartphone. These systems function effectively because they combine extensive data about human speech patterns with sophisticated algorithms for processing this information. They have access to data about how words sound in different accents and contexts, along with algorithms for converting speech to text. They combine data about common questions and phrases with algorithms for understanding meaning. They utilize data about various topics with algorithms for finding relevant information and forming appropriate responses.

Understanding this foundation helps us grasp both why AI systems need so much data to work effectively and why they perform best on specific, well-defined tasks. It also helps explain why AI systems can sometimes make mistakes, they can only work with the data they've been given and can only follow their algorithmic instructions.

As we move forward to explore more specific aspects of AI technology in later chapters, this understanding of data and algorithms will help us appreciate both the technical details and the practical implications of artificial intelligence systems.

As we conclude our exploration of AI fundamentals, let's connect the pieces we've discovered. We've seen that artificial intelligence isn't a single technology, but rather a combination of components working together to perform tasks that typically require human intelligence.

Think of an orchestra. Each instrument, strings, woodwinds, brass, and percussion, contributes its unique sound. When combined under proper direction, these individual elements create a symphony. Similarly, the components of AI we've explored each play their distinct roles while working together to create functioning AI systems.

Machine learning provides the ability to improve through experience, much like musicians getting better through practice. Neural networks offer pattern recognition capabilities, similar to how our brains recognize musical patterns in songs. Natural language processing enables communication between humans and machines, like the connection between a conductor and orchestra. All of these elements rely on the foundation of data and algorithms, just as music relies on notes and rules of composition.

We experience this harmony of AI components in everyday situations. When you talk to the virtual assistant on your smartphone, you're engaging with an intricate dance of technologies. Natural language processing works to understand your words, while machine learning continuously improves response accuracy. Neural networks process the patterns in your speech, while data and algorithms work together behind the scenes to generate appropriate responses.

Understanding these basics helps us better appreciate both what AI can and cannot do. Current AI excels at specific tasks when provided with good data and appropriate algorithms. It can recognize patterns, learn from examples, and communicate in increasingly natural ways. However, it doesn't think the way humans do, and it doesn't possess the general intelligence that humans have naturally.

This fundamental understanding provides a foundation for exploring more specific aspects of AI technology in the chapters ahead. As we delve deeper into different types of AI, examine specific technologies, and explore various applications, we'll build upon these basic concepts. Each new topic will connect back to these foundational ideas while adding new layers of understanding.

Our journey through AI's basics also prepares us to think critically about AI developments and applications. When we hear about new AI capabilities or applications, we can better evaluate them by considering what type of learning is involved, what patterns the system is recognizing, how it processes and responds to information, and what data and algorithms drive its performance.

As artificial intelligence continues to evolve and impact more aspects of our lives, this basic understanding becomes increasingly valuable. It helps us move beyond both unwarranted fears and unrealistic expectations, allowing us to see AI for what it is: a powerful tool that, when properly understood and applied, can enhance human capabilities and solve complex problems.

In the chapters ahead, we'll explore how these basic principles manifest in increasingly sophisticated ways, from different types of AI to core technologies and practical applications. Throughout our journey, we'll remember that even the most complex AI systems build upon these fundamental elements.

CHAPTER 4: TYPES OF AI

Having explored the basic components of artificial intelligence, machine learning, neural networks, and natural language processing, we now turn to understanding the different types of AI systems. Just as we classify living things into distinct categories to better understand them, categorizing AI helps us grasp its current capabilities, limitations, and future potential.

The world of artificial intelligence spans a remarkable spectrum, from highly specialized systems that excel at specific tasks to theoretical forms of AI that might one day match or exceed human intelligence across all domains. Understanding these categories proves crucial for anyone seeking to grasp AI's current reality and future possibilities.

Think of this spectrum like the progression of human tools throughout history. Early tools served specific purposes, a hammer for driving nails, a saw for cutting wood. More sophisticated tools combined multiple functions, like a Swiss Army knife. Finally, we might imagine future tools that could transform themselves into whatever we need. AI follows a similar pattern of development, from specialized tools to increasingly versatile systems.

Today's AI landscape is dominated by systems designed for specific tasks. These narrow AI applications surround us, from the predictive text on our smartphones to sophisticated medical diagnosis tools. While remarkably capable within their domains, these systems operate within clear boundaries. A chess-playing AI, no matter how brilliant at chess, cannot suddenly switch to driving a car or composing music.

Beyond these specialized systems lies the concept of general AI, machines that could match human intelligence across any domain. While this remains in the realm of research and theory, understanding its potential helps us appreciate both how far AI has come and how far it might go. Even further on the spectrum lies the concept of superintelligent AI, systems that could potentially surpass human capabilities in virtually every domain.

These categories, narrow, general, and super AI, provide more than just a classification system. They offer a framework for understanding the evolution of artificial intelligence, from today's practical applications to tomorrow's possibilities. This framework helps us evaluate new AI developments, understand their significance, and anticipate future directions in the field.

As we explore each category in detail, we'll see how our understanding of AI's basic components, which we developed in the previous chapter, manifests in different ways across this spectrum. We'll examine how today's narrow AI systems implement machine learning, neural networks, and natural language processing to achieve remarkable results within their specialized domains. We'll also consider how these same components might eventually contribute to the development of more general AI capabilities.

Let's begin our exploration with narrow AI, the type we interact with daily, before venturing into the more theoretical realms of general and super AI. This journey will deepen our understanding of both current AI capabilities and future possibilities, while helping us maintain a realistic perspective on artificial intelligence's evolution.

The artificial intelligence we encounter in our daily lives represents what we call narrow AI, systems designed and trained for specific tasks or limited domains. While these systems might perform their designated functions with remarkable proficiency, often exceeding human capabilities in their specific areas, they operate within clearly defined boundaries.

Consider language translation tools, which exemplify narrow AI at work. These systems can rapidly translate text between hundreds of language pairs, often handling complex idioms and context with impressive accuracy. Yet the same AI system that excels at translation cannot suddenly switch to diagnosing medical conditions or playing chess. This specialization defines narrow AI, exceptional capability within specific boundaries.

The power of narrow AI lies in its focused application. In healthcare, AI systems analyze medical images with remarkable precision, often detecting subtle patterns that might escape even experienced physicians. These same systems, however sophisticated in their medical analysis, cannot help with legal research or financial planning. Each application represents a specialized tool, much like a master craftsman's instruments, perfect for its intended use but unsuitable for tasks outside its domain.

We experience narrow AI's capabilities throughout our daily routines. When our email program filters spam from our inbox, it employs narrow AI trained specifically for that purpose. Our smartphone's facial recognition system uses narrow AI focused solely on identifying faces. Navigation apps use narrow AI to analyze traffic patterns and suggest optimal routes. Each of these applications demonstrates both the power and the limitations of narrow AI, exceptional performance within specific parameters.

The business world has embraced narrow AI's potential across numerous domains. In manufacturing, AI systems monitor production lines, identifying defects with superhuman accuracy. Financial institutions use specialized AI to detect fraudulent transactions in real-time. Customer service systems employ narrow AI to handle routine inquiries, freeing human agents for more complex interactions. Each application represents a carefully defined use of artificial intelligence for specific purposes.

Even in creative fields, narrow AI has found its niche. Music streaming services use specialized AI to analyze listening patterns and suggest songs. Gaming systems employ narrow AI to create more engaging opponent behaviors. Digital art tools use AI to enhance images or generate new ones based on specific parameters. Yet each of these creative applications remains confined to its particular domain.

Understanding narrow AI's nature helps explain both its current successes and limitations. These systems achieve their remarkable performance through intensive training in specific domains, using vast amounts of relevant data. A medical diagnosis AI system, for instance, might train on millions of medical images, becoming extraordinarily proficient at identifying specific conditions. This focused training enables exceptional performance but also defines the system's boundaries.

The specialization of narrow AI reflects our current technological capabilities. Rather than trying to create systems that can do everything, we've found remarkable success in developing AI that does specific things extraordinarily well. This approach has led to practical, valuable applications across numerous fields, from science and medicine to entertainment and daily convenience.

As artificial intelligence continues to develop, narrow AI systems become increasingly sophisticated within their domains. They improve their performance, handle greater complexity, and tackle more nuanced tasks. Yet they remain fundamentally narrow, powerful within their boundaries but unable to generalize their capabilities beyond them.

This reality of narrow AI sets the stage for understanding why achieving more general artificial intelligence presents such a significant challenge. The leap from specialized capability to general intelligence requires more than just improving existing systems, it requires a fundamental shift in how AI systems learn, adapt, and apply their capabilities across domains.

Moving beyond the specialized capabilities of narrow AI, we encounter a more ambitious concept: artificial general intelligence, or AGI. While narrow AI excels at specific tasks, general AI represents something far more comprehensive, systems that could match human intelligence across any domain. This represents not just a difference in capability, but a fundamental shift in the nature of artificial intelligence.

Think about how human intelligence works. We can learn to play chess, then apply our problem-solving abilities to learn cooking, or writing, or mathematics. We adapt our knowledge and skills to new situations, recognize patterns across different domains, and approach unfamiliar challenges with creativity and insight. This versatility defines human intelligence, and represents what general AI aims to achieve.

Unlike today's specialized AI systems, general AI would be able to understand, learn, and apply intelligence in ways that mirror human cognitive capabilities. It would not need to be specifically programmed or trained for each new task. Instead, like humans, it would be able to learn from experience, apply knowledge across domains, and adapt to new situations.

For example, while a narrow AI system might excel at playing Go or chess, a general AI system would be able to learn and play any game, understanding the principles of strategy and competition that apply across different types of games. More importantly, it could apply insights gained from game-playing to entirely different domains, just as humans do.

This ability to transfer knowledge and skills across domains represents one of the key characteristics that would distinguish general AI from our current narrow AI systems. A general AI system learning about architecture might apply principles from nature, mathematics, and art, drawing connections that inform its understanding and creativity, much as human architects do.

However, general AI remains theoretical. Despite significant advances in artificial intelligence, we have not yet created systems that can truly match human cognitive flexibility. Our most sophisticated AI systems, while impressive in their specific domains, still operate within the bounds of narrow AI, unable to transfer their capabilities beyond their trained specialties.

Understanding this gap between current reality and the goal of general AI helps explain both the challenges and potential of artificial intelligence. The development of AGI would require not just more powerful systems or better algorithms, but fundamentally new approaches to how machines learn, reason, and understand the world.

The implications of achieving general AI would be profound. Systems with human-level intelligence across all domains could contribute to solving complex challenges in science, medicine, engineering, and virtually every field of human endeavor. They could work alongside humans, bringing complementary capabilities and perspectives to problem-solving and innovation.

Yet the development of general AI also raises important questions about the relationship between human and machine intelligence. Would such systems truly think as we do? Would they have consciousness or self-awareness? These questions move beyond technical considerations into philosophical territory, touching on fundamental questions about the nature of intelligence and consciousness itself.

For now, general AI remains a goal rather than a reality. While researchers continue to push the boundaries of what artificial intelligence can achieve, the gap between narrow and general AI reminds us of both the remarkable progress we've made and the significant challenges that lie ahead in the development of artificial intelligence.

At the furthest end of the AI spectrum lies a concept that pushes the boundaries of our imagination: superintelligent AI. While narrow AI represents today's reality and general AI remains a future goal, super AI ventures into territory that exists primarily in theoretical discussions and scientific exploration, artificial intelligence that would surpass human capabilities not just in specific areas, but in virtually every domain.

To understand super AI, imagine an intelligence that combines the specialization of narrow AI with the flexibility of general AI, but operating at levels far beyond human capacity. Such a system would not only match human abilities in areas like scientific research, creative thinking, and problem-solving, it would exceed them, potentially discovering solutions and insights that human intelligence alone could not achieve.

The theoretical capabilities of super AI extend far beyond what we can currently envision. While today's narrow AI might process data faster than humans in specific domains, super AI would demonstrate superior cognitive abilities across all areas. It might solve complex scientific problems, generate revolutionary technological innovations, and address challenges that have long puzzled human researchers, all while continuing to learn and improve its own capabilities.

This concept of self-improvement represents one of the most intriguing and challenging aspects of super AI. Unlike current AI systems that require human intervention to upgrade or improve, a superintelligent AI might be capable of enhancing its own algorithms and capabilities. This theoretical ability to self-improve raises both exciting possibilities and important questions about control and development.

However, we must maintain perspective when discussing super AI. While it captures imagination and drives some long-term research goals, it remains firmly in the theoretical realm. We have not yet achieved general AI, making super AI a concept that lies even further in the future. Understanding super AI helps us think about the ultimate potential of artificial intelligence, but it should not distract from the more immediate developments and challenges in the field.

The concept of super AI also raises profound questions about the relationship between human and machine intelligence. How would human society interact with intelligence that surpasses our own capabilities? What role would humans play in a world where machines could solve problems more effectively than we can? These questions, while theoretical, help us think about the long-term implications of AI development.

The development path toward super AI, if it ever occurs, would likely be gradual rather than sudden. Just as the journey from narrow to general AI requires fundamental breakthroughs, the step from general to super AI would involve advances we can currently only speculate about. This perspective helps ground our understanding of AI's potential future while maintaining focus on current developments and challenges.

Understanding how these three types of AI, narrow, general, and super, relate to each other helps clarify both the current state and potential future of artificial intelligence. Each type represents not just different levels of capability, but fundamentally different approaches to machine intelligence.

Think of these three types as points along a journey. Narrow AI, our current reality, excels within specific boundaries. Like a skilled craftsperson who masters one trade, these systems achieve remarkable results within their specialized domains. A chess-playing AI might outperform grandmasters, while a medical diagnosis system might detect patterns that elude human experts. Yet neither can apply its capabilities outside its trained domain.

General AI represents a quantum leap forward, the difference between a specialist and a Renaissance person who excels across many fields. This theoretical advancement would bridge the gap between specialized and universal capability, creating systems that could, like humans, learn and adapt across any domain. The jump from narrow to general AI isn't just about increasing power or capability; it requires a fundamental shift in how machines learn and apply knowledge.

Super AI takes this progression even further, suggesting systems that would surpass human capability not just in specific areas, but in virtually every domain. If narrow AI is like a master craftsperson and general AI like a Renaissance genius, super AI would represent an intelligence beyond anything humanity has encountered, capable of insights and achievements we might struggle to comprehend.

The progression from one type to another involves more than just increased processing power or better algorithms. Each step requires fundamental breakthroughs in how machines process information, learn from experience, and apply knowledge. The gap between today's narrow AI and theoretical general AI isn't just a matter of scale, it represents a qualitative shift in the nature of machine intelligence.

Looking at these types together reveals important patterns in AI development. Narrow AI demonstrates that machines can indeed exhibit intelligence, albeit within specific boundaries. The theoretical framework of general AI suggests that these boundaries might eventually be overcome. Super AI represents the ultimate extension of this progression, raising both exciting possibilities and important questions about the future of intelligence itself.

This understanding helps us maintain perspective when evaluating AI developments. New AI capabilities, no matter how impressive, currently operate within the realm of narrow AI. While these advances push the boundaries of what specialized systems can achieve, they don't necessarily bring us closer to general AI. Each type of AI represents a distinct paradigm, with its own challenges and implications.

The relationship between these types also helps us

understand the challenges ahead. Moving from narrow to general AI isn't simply a matter of making existing systems more powerful, it requires fundamentally new approaches to how machines learn and understand. Similarly, the leap from general to super AI would involve advances we can currently only theorize about.

This progression reminds us that while artificial intelligence has made remarkable strides, we're still in the early stages of its potential development. Today's narrow AI systems, impressive as they are, represent just the beginning of what might be possible as the field continues to evolve.

As we consider the progression from narrow to general to super AI, we must understand what this development path might look like. While science fiction often depicts sudden leaps in artificial intelligence, reality suggests a more gradual evolution, with each advance building upon previous developments while facing its own unique challenges.

Today's path forward begins with expanding the capabilities of narrow AI. While these systems remain specialized, they continue to take on increasingly complex tasks within their domains. Medical diagnosis systems learn to analyze more conditions, language systems handle more nuanced communication, and visual recognition systems identify more subtle patterns. These advances, while impressive, still operate within the fundamental framework of narrow AI, specialized systems for specific purposes.

The journey toward general AI represents a far more complex challenge. Unlike the incremental improvements we see in narrow AI, achieving general AI requires solving fundamental questions about the nature of intelligence itself. How do humans transfer knowledge between different domains? How do we apply past experiences to new situations? How do we combine different types of understanding to solve novel problems? These questions hint at the magnitude of the challenge in creating truly general artificial intelligence.

Consider how a child learns to understand the world. They don't just memorize facts or follow predetermined rules, they develop an intuitive understanding that they can apply across different situations. This ability to learn, adapt, and apply knowledge flexibly represents the kind of intelligence that general AI would need to achieve. The gap between our current specialized systems and this level of adaptive intelligence remains vast.

The theoretical path to super AI appears even more challenging. While we can observe human intelligence as a model for general AI, super AI would venture into territory beyond human capability. This makes its development path particularly difficult to envision. How do we create systems that surpass human intelligence when human intelligence represents our primary model for understanding intelligence itself?

These challenges remind us to maintain realistic expectations about AI's development. While progress continues in expanding the capabilities of narrow AI, the fundamental breakthroughs needed for general AI, let alone super AI, remain elusive. This doesn't diminish the remarkable achievements in current AI development, but rather helps us understand them in proper context.

Understanding this development path also helps us appreciate why certain challenges prove particularly difficult. Tasks that humans perform easily, like generalizing knowledge from one domain to another or understanding context in communication, often prove surprisingly challenging for AI systems. These challenges reveal the complexity of intelligence itself, whether natural or artificial.

As we look to the future, this understanding helps guide our expectations and preparations. While we continue to develop and deploy more sophisticated narrow AI systems, we can also work to understand the fundamental challenges that lie ahead. This might involve not just technical development, but deeper research into the nature of intelligence, learning, and consciousness itself.

As we conclude our exploration of AI types, we find ourselves at an interesting moment in the evolution of artificial intelligence. We understand that narrow AI, despite its limitations, continues to achieve remarkable results in specific domains. We can envision the transformative potential of general AI, even as it remains theoretical. And we can contemplate the profound implications of super AI, while recognizing it exists primarily in the realm of future possibility.

This understanding of AI types provides crucial context for evaluating both current developments and future possibilities. When we hear about new AI breakthroughs, we can place them within this framework. Is this an advancement in narrow AI, pushing the boundaries of what specialized systems can achieve? Or does it represent a step toward the more fundamental capabilities needed for general AI? This perspective helps us maintain both optimism about AI's potential and realism about its current state.

Our journey through these different types of AI also reveals important truths about the nature of intelligence itself. The challenges in moving from narrow to general AI highlight the remarkable complexity of human intelligence, our ability to learn, adapt, and apply knowledge across domains. Even as we work to recreate aspects of intelligence in machines, we gain deeper appreciation for the sophistication of natural intelligence.

Looking ahead, we can expect continued rapid progress in narrow AI applications. These systems will become more sophisticated, tackle more complex tasks, and find new applications across various fields. Yet they will remain fundamentally narrow, specialized tools rather than general intelligence. Understanding this helps set appropriate expectations for AI development in the near future.

The pursuit of general AI will likely continue as a long-term research goal, driving fundamental investigations into the nature of intelligence and learning. While we may be far from achieving general AI, the quest to create it pushes us to better understand how intelligence works, how knowledge transfers between domains, and how adaptive learning occurs. These insights prove valuable even if general AI remains elusive.

As we move forward in our exploration of artificial intelligence, this understanding of AI types provides a foundation for deeper investigation of specific technologies and applications. In the coming chapters, we'll examine the technical elements that power current AI systems, always keeping in mind where these developments fit within the broader spectrum of AI capabilities.

The distinction between narrow, general, and super AI reminds us that artificial intelligence remains a field in evolution. Today's achievements, while impressive, represent early steps in a longer journey. By understanding these different types of AI, we better appreciate both current capabilities and future possibilities, while maintaining a realistic perspective about the challenges and opportunities that lie ahead.

GIL OREN

CHAPTER 5: INSIDE AI TECHNOLOGIES

Having explored the different types of artificial intelligence, from today's narrow AI to theoretical superintelligent systems, we now turn our attention to the technologies that make current AI possible. Three core technologies form the foundation of modern artificial intelligence: machine learning, neural networks, and natural language processing.

These technologies work together to create the AI systems we encounter daily. While Chapter 3 introduced these concepts broadly, we'll now examine them in greater detail, understanding not just what they do but how they function and interact. This deeper understanding proves crucial for anyone seeking to grasp the true capabilities and limitations of artificial intelligence.

Think of these technologies as the engine, transmission, and control systems of AI. Machine learning provides the fundamental ability to improve through experience, much as an engine provides power to a vehicle. Neural networks offer sophisticated pattern recognition capabilities, like a

73

transmission system translating power into specific types of movement. Natural language processing enables communication between humans and machines, similar to how control systems allow us to direct a vehicle's power and movement.

Understanding these technologies helps explain both the remarkable achievements and current limitations of artificial intelligence. Each technology brings unique capabilities, and their combination enables increasingly sophisticated applications. When we use a virtual assistant, for instance, we engage with all three technologies working in concert: natural language processing interprets our words, neural networks recognize patterns in our speech, and machine learning helps the system improve its responses over time.

Yet these technologies also have distinct characteristics and limitations. Machine learning requires appropriate data and training. Neural networks need proper structure and optimization. Natural language processing must navigate the complexities of human communication. Understanding these aspects helps us better appreciate both what current AI can achieve and what challenges it faces.

This exploration proves particularly relevant as AI continues to evolve. New applications emerge regularly, pushing the boundaries of what these technologies can accomplish. By understanding the fundamental technologies, we can better evaluate these developments and their potential impact.

As we delve into each technology, we'll maintain focus on practical understanding rather than technical complexity. Our goal is to understand these technologies well enough to appreciate their capabilities, limitations, and potential, while avoiding the technical details that belong in more specialized texts.

Let's begin with machine learning, the technology that enables AI systems to learn from experience rather than following fixed programming. This fundamental capability underlies many of modern AI's most impressive achievements and continues to drive innovation across numerous fields.

Machine learning represents perhaps the most fundamental shift in how computers approach tasks. Traditional computer programs follow explicit instructions: if this happens, do that. Machine learning takes a different approach, enabling systems to learn from experience and improve their performance over time.

Consider how you learned to recognize cats. No one gave you a detailed list of measurements or mathematical formulas defining "cat." Instead, you saw many examples of cats in different situations until you could reliably identify them. Machine learning works similarly, learning from examples rather than following predetermined rules.

This ability to learn from data dramatically expands what computers can achieve. Rather than requiring programmers to anticipate and code for every possible situation, machine learning systems can discover patterns and adapt to new scenarios. This flexibility proves crucial for tasks where writing explicit rules would be impractical or impossible.

Machine learning systems employ three main approaches to learning, each suited to different types of tasks and situations.

Supervised learning occurs when systems learn from labeled examples. Imagine teaching a child to identify letters. You might show them the letter "A" and say "This is A" many times until they learn to recognize it. Similarly, supervised learning systems train on data where the correct answers are known. An email spam filter, for instance, learns from millions of messages already labeled as spam or not spam.

Unsupervised learning involves finding patterns in data without labeled examples. Think of how you might notice that your friends naturally fall into different social groups, even without anyone explicitly defining these groups. Unsupervised learning systems similarly discover patterns and structures within data. Streaming services use this approach to group viewers with similar tastes, helping them make better recommendations.

Reinforcement learning teaches systems through experience and feedback. Consider how a child learns to ride a bicycle, receiving immediate feedback through success or failure. Reinforcement learning systems similarly learn by taking actions and receiving feedback about their results. This approach proves particularly valuable in robotics and game playing, where systems can learn optimal strategies through practice.

Machine learning touches almost every aspect of modern life. When your credit card company prevents fraud, it uses machine learning systems trained on millions of transactions to spot suspicious activity. Navigation apps learn from traffic patterns to predict the fastest routes. Medical systems learn from thousands of images to help detect diseases in x-rays and scans.

The power of machine learning lies in its ability to find patterns in large amounts of data. While humans excel at learning from a few examples, machine learning systems can analyze millions of examples to find subtle patterns we might miss. This capability makes them particularly valuable for tasks involving large datasets or complex patterns.

However, machine learning systems also have important limitations. They can only learn from the data they receive, which means they might perpetuate biases present in their training data. They typically perform well only on tasks similar to what they were trained for, lacking the flexible intelligence humans possess. Understanding these limitations proves as important as appreciating their capabilities.

As we look toward the future, machine learning continues to evolve. New techniques emerge regularly, expanding what these systems can achieve. Yet the fundamental principle remains the same: learning from data to improve performance over time.

If machine learning represents the foundation of modern

AI BASICS: THE FUNDAMENTALS

AI, neural networks provide its most sophisticated architecture. These systems take inspiration from the human brain's structure, creating artificial networks that can recognize complex patterns in data. The term "deep learning" refers to neural networks with multiple layers, capable of processing information with increasing levels of abstraction.

Our brains contain billions of neurons connected in intricate networks, each neuron receiving and sending signals to others. Artificial neural networks mirror this structure in simplified form. They consist of interconnected nodes, or artificial neurons, organized in layers. Each connection can strengthen or weaken over time, much like biological neural pathways adjust as we learn.

Picture how you recognize a friend's face. Your brain processes visual information through multiple stages, from identifying basic shapes and colors to recognizing specific features to finally achieving recognition. Artificial neural networks operate similarly, processing information through successive layers to arrive at conclusions.

The "deep" in deep learning refers to the multiple layers through which information passes. Each layer extracts different features from the input data, building increasingly sophisticated understanding. In an image recognition system, early layers might detect simple edges and shapes, middle layers might identify features like eyes or noses, and deeper layers combine these features to recognize complete faces.

This layered approach gives deep learning systems remarkable capabilities. They can learn to recognize patterns too complex for traditional programming approaches. When you unlock your phone with your face, deep learning networks analyze the image, accounting for different angles, lighting conditions, and even changes in your appearance.

The impact of neural networks extends far beyond facial recognition. Medical systems use deep learning to analyze medical images, often detecting subtle signs of disease that human doctors might miss. Translation services employ neural networks to understand context and nuance in different languages. Self-driving cars use them to interpret their environment, identifying everything from traffic signs to pedestrians.

In creative fields, neural networks demonstrate surprising capabilities. They can generate realistic images from text descriptions, create music in different styles, or even assist in drug discovery by predicting molecular properties. These applications show how deep learning can find patterns and create outputs in ways that sometimes appear almost human-like.

However, neural networks also face distinct challenges. They require substantial amounts of data for training and significant computing power to operate effectively. Their decision-making processes can be difficult to interpret, raising concerns in applications where understanding the reasoning behind decisions proves crucial. Additionally, like other AI systems, they can reflect biases present in their training data.

Understanding these strengths and limitations helps explain both the current capabilities and future potential of neural networks. As computing power increases and new architectures emerge, these systems continue to advance, taking on increasingly complex tasks while maintaining their fundamental approach of learning through layered pattern recognition.

Natural Language Processing (NLP) represents one of artificial intelligence's most remarkable achievements: enabling machines to understand and interact with human language. While machine learning provides the learning capability and neural networks offer pattern recognition, NLP applies these technologies to the specific challenge of human communication.

Human language presents unique challenges for computers. We speak and write with nuance, context, and implied meaning. A simple phrase like "I'm feeling blue" might indicate sadness rather than color, requiring understanding beyond literal definitions. NLP systems must navigate these complexities to interpret and generate human language effectively.

Consider how you understand language. You process not just individual words but grammar, context, tone, and cultural references. NLP systems approach this task systematically, breaking down language into components they can analyze. They examine everything from the basic structure of sentences to the relationships between words to the broader context of communication.

Modern NLP systems can perform an impressive array of tasks. When you speak to your smartphone's virtual assistant, NLP converts your speech to text, interprets your meaning, formulates an appropriate response, and converts that response back to speech. Each step requires sophisticated processing of language.

Translation services showcase another aspect of NLP capability. These systems must understand not just vocabulary but grammar, idioms, and cultural context in both languages. While not perfect, they can effectively translate between hundreds of language pairs, making global communication more accessible than ever.

Text analysis represents another crucial application. NLP systems can analyze customer feedback to gauge sentiment, process legal documents to extract key information, or summarize long texts into brief overviews. These capabilities prove increasingly valuable as organizations deal with growing volumes of text-based information.

NLP appears in countless applications we use daily. Email systems use it to filter spam and categorize messages. Search engines employ it to understand our queries and find relevant results. Social media platforms use it to moderate content and identify trending topics.

In professional settings, NLP enables new forms of automation and assistance. Customer service systems can handle routine inquiries, freeing human agents for more complex issues. Document processing systems can extract information from forms and reports. Meeting transcription services can convert spoken conversations into searchable text.

However, current NLP systems still face significant limitations. They can struggle with ambiguity, sarcasm, and complex context. They might miss subtle meanings that humans grasp intuitively. Understanding these limitations helps set realistic expectations for NLP applications while appreciating their genuine capabilities.

The development of NLP continues to advance rapidly. New techniques and more powerful models emerge regularly, expanding what these systems can achieve. Yet the fundamental challenge remains the same: bridging the gap between human communication and machine processing.

Understanding each AI technology individually reveals only part of the picture. The true power of modern artificial intelligence emerges when these technologies combine and complement each other. Most AI applications we encounter rely not on a single technology but on the sophisticated interplay between multiple components.

Consider what happens when you ask your smartphone's virtual assistant about the weather. Natural language processing interprets your spoken words, converting them to text and understanding your request. Machine learning systems, trained on millions of similar interactions, help determine the most appropriate response. Neural networks process your speech patterns and help generate natural-sounding replies.

This integration extends to more complex applications. In autonomous vehicles, machine learning systems trained on traffic patterns work alongside neural networks processing visual information from cameras. Natural language processing enables voice commands and provides spoken notifications. Each technology contributes its strengths to create a comprehensive system.

Medical diagnosis systems demonstrate another powerful integration of these technologies. Machine learning algorithms analyze patient histories and symptoms. Neural networks process medical images like X-rays or MRIs. Natural language processing helps interpret doctors' notes and medical literature. Together, these technologies can assist healthcare professionals in making more informed decisions.

In financial services, similar cooperation occurs. Machine learning systems detect fraudulent transactions by analyzing patterns. Neural networks process complex market data to identify trends. Natural language processing analyzes news reports and financial documents. The combination helps financial institutions protect customers and make better investment decisions.

Even creative applications benefit from this technological synergy. Content creation systems combine natural language processing to understand style and context, neural networks to generate appropriate content, and machine learning to improve based on feedback. These systems can help with everything from writing assistance to music composition.

However, this integration also presents challenges. Each technology brings its own limitations and potential biases. Systems must coordinate effectively while maintaining reliability. Understanding these challenges helps explain both current capabilities and areas needing improvement.

The future of AI likely involves even deeper integration of these technologies. As each component advances, their combined capabilities grow. Yet success depends not just on individual technological progress but on better ways of combining these technologies effectively.

Understanding the core technologies of AI helps us assess where the field truly stands today. While media headlines often focus on the most dramatic achievements or theoretical possibilities, a clear understanding of current capabilities and limitations proves essential for realistic evaluation of AI systems.

Machine learning systems today excel at finding patterns in structured data and improving specific tasks through experience. From fraud detection to product recommendations, these systems demonstrate remarkable capabilities within their defined domains. However, they remain fundamentally tied to their training data and specified objectives, lacking the flexible learning abilities humans possess naturally.

Neural networks and deep learning have achieved impressive results in pattern recognition tasks. Image recognition often matches or exceeds human performance in specific applications. Speech recognition works reliably enough for everyday use. Yet these systems still require extensive training data and can make surprising errors when encountering situations that differ significantly from their training.

Natural language processing continues to advance rapidly. Modern systems can engage in increasingly natural conversations, translate between languages with growing accuracy, and analyze text with remarkable sophistication. However, they still struggle with nuanced understanding, complex context, and truly natural communication.

Implementing AI technologies in real-world situations reveals both their power and their practical limitations. While AI systems can process vast amounts of data and recognize complex patterns, they require careful setup, appropriate data, and ongoing maintenance. Success depends not just on the technology itself but on how well it fits specific use cases and organizational needs.

Current AI systems work best when their objectives are clearly defined and their domains well understood. A system designed to detect fraudulent transactions can perform remarkably well, while one attempting to engage in open-ended problem solving might struggle. Understanding these boundaries helps organizations implement AI effectively.

AI BASICS: THE FUNDAMENTALS

The need for quality data remains crucial. AI systems can only learn from the information they receive, and their performance depends heavily on the quality and representativeness of their training data. Organizations must consider not just the technology but the data infrastructure needed to support it.

As we look at the current state of AI, we see a technology that has achieved remarkable capabilities in specific areas while still facing significant limitations in others. This understanding helps guide both current implementation decisions and future development efforts.

Our exploration of AI technologies reveals a field in constant evolution. Understanding the current capabilities and limitations of machine learning, neural networks, and natural language processing helps us anticipate future developments and prepare for continued advancement in artificial intelligence.

The path forward for these technologies appears both exciting and challenging. Machine learning continues to find new applications and approaches, pushing the boundaries of what systems can learn from data. Researchers explore ways to make learning more efficient, requiring less data and computing power while achieving better results.

Neural networks grow more sophisticated, with new architectures emerging regularly. Advances in computing power enable larger, more complex networks capable of tackling increasingly challenging tasks. These developments suggest continued improvements in areas like image recognition, speech processing, and pattern identification.

Natural language processing moves toward more nuanced understanding of human communication. Systems improve at grasping context, maintaining coherent conversations, and generating appropriate responses. This progress points toward more natural and effective human-machine interaction.

These advances carry important implications for how we work and live. Organizations must prepare for increasingly capable AI systems while understanding their practical limitations. This means developing strategies that leverage AI's strengths while accounting for its constraints.

Education and training need to evolve alongside these technologies. Understanding AI becomes increasingly important not just for technical specialists but for anyone working with or affected by these systems. This includes understanding both capabilities and limitations to make informed decisions about AI implementation and use.

The future likely holds both expected and surprising developments. While we can anticipate continued improvement in current applications, new capabilities and applications will likely emerge as these technologies mature and combine in novel ways.

As we conclude our examination of AI technologies, we carry forward crucial insights about their nature and potential. These insights will prove valuable as we explore more specific applications and implications in the chapters ahead. Understanding the technological foundation helps us better appreciate both current capabilities and future possibilities while maintaining realistic expectations about artificial intelligence's development..

CHAPTER 6: THE MECHANICS OF AI

Having explored the core technologies that power artificial intelligence, we now turn to understanding how these systems actually work. While the previous chapter introduced machine learning, neural networks, and natural language processing, this chapter examines the fundamental mechanics that make these technologies function: data, algorithms, and the training process.

Think of artificial intelligence like a car. In the previous chapter, we learned about different types of engines, transmission systems, and control mechanisms. Now we'll look under the hood to understand how these components work together. This practical understanding proves essential for anyone seeking to work with or implement AI systems effectively.

The mechanics of AI involve three essential elements working in concert. Data provides the raw material from which AI systems learn. Algorithms process this data and make decisions. Training brings these elements together, enabling systems to learn and improve over time.

Understanding these mechanics helps explain both the capabilities and limitations of current AI systems.

Data forms the foundation of every AI system. Just as a car needs fuel to run, AI systems need data to learn and operate. However, not all data serves equally well. Understanding what makes good training data, how much data systems need, and how data quality affects performance proves crucial for successful AI implementation.

Algorithms serve as the engine of AI systems, processing data to produce results. Different types of algorithms suit different tasks, each with its own strengths and limitations. Knowledge of these differences helps in selecting the right approach for specific applications.

The training process brings data and algorithms together, enabling systems to learn from experience. This process requires careful attention to multiple factors, from data preparation to performance validation. Understanding these elements helps explain why some AI systems succeed while others struggle.

These mechanics underlie every AI application we encounter. When your email system filters spam, it applies algorithms trained on vast amounts of message data. When your smartphone recognizes your face, it uses algorithms trained on numerous facial images. When virtual assistants understand your requests, they rely on algorithms trained on extensive language data.

As we explore these mechanics in detail, we'll see how theoretical concepts translate into practical applications. This understanding proves valuable whether you're implementing AI systems, working with AI tools, or simply wanting to better understand how these technologies function in the real world.

Data serves as the foundation of every artificial intelligence system. Without data, even the most sophisticated algorithms remain powerless. Understanding the role of data, its characteristics, and how it affects AI system performance proves essential for grasping how these systems work.

AI BASICS: THE FUNDAMENTALS

AI systems learn from many types of data. Text data enables language understanding and generation. Image data powers visual recognition systems. Numerical data drives prediction and analysis. Sound data enables speech recognition and processing. Each type of data requires specific preparation and handling for effective use.

The quality of this data directly impacts system performance. Consider teaching a child to read. Showing them clear, well-written text works better than smudged or incorrect writing. Similarly, AI systems learn best from clean, accurate, and relevant data. Poor quality data leads to poor performance, no matter how sophisticated the underlying system.

While AI systems often benefit from large amounts of data, quantity alone proves insufficient. A balance between quantity and quality determines success. A smaller dataset of high-quality examples often produces better results than a larger collection of poor-quality data.

Quality factors include accuracy, relevance, and representation. Accurate data contains correct information without errors or inconsistencies. Relevant data relates directly to the intended task. Representative data covers the full range of situations the system might encounter.

Consider an AI system learning to recognize medical conditions in x-rays. It needs clear images, correct diagnosis labels, and examples of both common and rare conditions. Missing any of these elements could lead to unreliable performance, regardless of the total number of images available.

In practical applications, data preparation often requires substantial effort. Organizations must collect appropriate data, clean it to remove errors, and format it for use. This process might involve combining data from multiple sources, handling missing information, or converting between formats.

The importance of data quality appears across all AI applications. Spam filters need accurately labeled examples of both spam and legitimate messages. Facial recognition systems need clear images from various angles and lighting conditions. Language systems need well-formed text in the languages they handle.

Data requirements also evolve as systems learn and improve. Initial training might require one type of data, while ongoing improvement needs additional examples of difficult or edge cases. Understanding these changing needs helps organizations plan for successful AI implementation.

If data provides the foundation for AI systems, algorithms serve as their engine, processing information and making decisions. An algorithm is simply a set of instructions that tells a system how to handle data and produce results. Understanding how algorithms work helps explain both the capabilities and limitations of AI systems.

Think of algorithms as recipes for processing information. Just as a cooking recipe converts ingredients into a finished dish, AI algorithms convert raw data into useful outputs. These "recipes" can range from simple decision rules to complex mathematical operations, but all serve the same basic purpose: transforming input data into meaningful results.

The power of AI algorithms lies in their ability to identify patterns and learn from experience. Unlike traditional computer programs that follow fixed rules, AI algorithms can adjust their behavior based on the data they process. This adaptability enables them to improve their performance over time.

Decision trees represent one of the most straightforward types of AI algorithms. They work by breaking complex decisions into series of simpler choices, much like a flow chart. In medical diagnosis applications, for instance, decision trees might evaluate symptoms one at a time to reach a conclusion about potential conditions.

Neural network algorithms process information through interconnected layers, similar to how human brains operate. When your smartphone recognizes your face, neural network algorithms analyze the image through successive stages, identifying features and patterns until reaching a final decision about whether the face matches stored examples.

The K-nearest neighbors algorithm makes decisions by comparing new situations to similar past examples. This approach powers many recommendation systems. When an online store suggests products you might like, it often uses this type of algorithm to find customers with similar preferences and recommend items they enjoyed.

Choosing the right algorithm for a specific task proves crucial for success. Different algorithms suit different types of problems. Decision trees work well for clear, rule-based decisions. Neural networks excel at pattern recognition in complex data. K-nearest neighbors algorithms perform best when similar past examples provide good guidance for new situations.

Real-world applications often combine multiple algorithms to achieve better results. A virtual assistant might use one algorithm to convert speech to text, another to understand the meaning of words, and a third to generate appropriate responses. Understanding these combinations helps explain how complex AI systems achieve their capabilities.

The effectiveness of any algorithm depends heavily on the quality and quantity of available data. Even the most sophisticated algorithm cannot produce good results from poor data. Similarly, simple algorithms sometimes outperform complex ones when provided with high-quality, relevant data.

With data as the foundation and algorithms as the engine, training represents the process that brings these elements together to create functional AI systems. Training determines how well an AI system performs its intended tasks, making it a crucial aspect of AI development.

Training an AI system resembles teaching a student. Just as students need examples, practice, and feedback to learn effectively, AI systems require properly structured data, repeated exposure to examples, and performance evaluation to develop their capabilities. This process transforms raw algorithms into useful tools for specific tasks.

Consider how you learned to recognize different breeds of dogs. You likely saw many examples, learned distinguishing features, and gradually improved your ability to identify breeds correctly. AI systems learn similarly, though they process information mathematically rather than through conscious understanding.

Supervised learning represents the most straightforward training approach. The system receives examples with correct answers, much like a student working through solved problems. A system learning to identify spam emails, for instance, processes thousands of messages already labeled as spam or legitimate, learning to recognize distinguishing characteristics.

Unsupervised learning works differently, with systems finding patterns in data without explicit guidance. This approach resembles asking students to group similar items without telling them the categories in advance. Customer segmentation systems, for example, might discover natural groupings in customer behavior without predefined classifications.

Reinforcement learning involves systems learning through trial and error with feedback about their performance. Like learning to play a game, the system tries different approaches, receives feedback about what works, and gradually improves its strategy. This method proves particularly valuable for tasks involving sequences of decisions.

The training process begins with data collection and preparation. This crucial first stage involves gathering appropriate data, cleaning it to remove errors or inconsistencies, and formatting it for use. The quality of this preparation directly affects training success.

During the actual training phase, systems process their training data repeatedly, adjusting their internal parameters to improve performance. This iterative process continues until the system achieves satisfactory results or shows no further improvement. The time required varies greatly depending on the task complexity and amount of data involved.

Validation and testing form the final stage, where systems demonstrate their capabilities on new data they haven't seen during training. This stage reveals how well systems will perform in real-world situations. Poor performance during validation often indicates problems with either the training data or the training process itself.

Understanding data, algorithms, and training separately provides crucial insights, but successful AI systems require these elements to work together seamlessly. The integration process determines how well these components combine to create effective solutions for real-world challenges.

Think of integration like orchestrating a performance. Each musician might play their part perfectly, but creating beautiful music requires careful coordination among all players. Similarly, AI systems need their components to work in harmony. Data must match algorithm requirements, training processes must suit both data and algorithms, and the entire system must align with its intended purpose.

Consider a practical example: a system that helps doctors identify potential diseases in medical images. The integration process ensures high-quality medical images flow properly into appropriate algorithms, training proceeds effectively with proper medical validation, and the system produces results in a format useful for healthcare professionals.

Integration often reveals practical challenges hidden when examining components separately. Data might arrive in unexpected formats. Algorithms might process information more slowly than anticipated. Training might require more time or computing resources than planned. Successful integration requires addressing these practical considerations.

System performance provides one crucial consideration. While individual components might work well in isolation, their combination needs to meet speed and accuracy requirements for practical use. A facial recognition system for smartphone unlocking, for instance, must work quickly and accurately enough for daily use.

Reliability presents another key challenge. Integrated systems must maintain consistent performance over time and across varying conditions. They need to handle unexpected inputs gracefully, manage resource constraints effectively, and provide consistent results for their users.

Resource requirements also affect integration success. Systems need appropriate computing power, storage capacity, and network capabilities. Understanding these requirements helps organizations plan effective implementations and avoid performance problems.

The integration process often reveals opportunities for improvement. Teams might discover better ways to prepare data, more efficient algorithms for specific tasks, or more effective training approaches. This ongoing refinement helps systems evolve and improve over time.

Understanding how AI systems work mechanically not only explains current capabilities but also helps us anticipate future developments. As data collection expands, algorithms improve, and training processes advance, new possibilities continue to emerge.

The mechanics of AI systems continue to evolve. New approaches to data processing promise to reduce the amount of training data needed for effective performance. This could make AI systems more practical for applications where large datasets prove difficult to obtain or maintain.

Algorithm development also advances steadily. Researchers explore ways to make algorithms more efficient, requiring less computing power while delivering better results. These improvements could enable more sophisticated AI applications on everyday devices, from smartphones to home appliances.

Training processes grow more sophisticated as well. New techniques help systems learn more effectively from limited examples or adapt more quickly to changing conditions. These advances could lead to AI systems that learn and improve more naturally, similar to how humans gain expertise through experience.

These developments carry important implications for organizations implementing AI solutions. Understanding the mechanics helps decision-makers plan effectively for future capabilities while managing current limitations. This knowledge proves particularly valuable when evaluating new AI technologies or planning system upgrades.

The relationship between data, algorithms, and training will likely remain fundamental to AI systems, even as specific approaches evolve. Organizations that understand these basics can better adapt to new developments and take advantage of emerging capabilities.

As we look ahead, the mechanics of AI remind us that progress often comes through incremental improvements rather than dramatic breakthroughs. Better data preparation methods, more efficient algorithms, and improved training processes combine to enable new applications and enhance existing ones.

In the chapters ahead, we'll explore how these mechanics translate into practical applications across various industries and domains. Understanding how AI systems work internally will help us better appreciate both their current impact and future potential.

GIL OREN

CHAPTER 7: AI IN EVERYDAY LIFE

Having explored the technologies and mechanics that power artificial intelligence, we now turn to its practical impact on our daily lives. AI has moved beyond research laboratories and specialized applications to become an integral part of how we work, communicate, and live. Understanding these practical applications helps us appreciate both current capabilities and future possibilities.

Artificial intelligence surrounds us in ways both obvious and subtle. When your smartphone recognizes your face or voice, you interact directly with AI. When your email program filters spam or your music service suggests songs, AI works quietly in the background. From morning alarms optimized for your sleep patterns to evening entertainment recommendations, AI shapes countless moments throughout our days.

This integration happened gradually, application by application. Tasks that once required human intervention now occur automatically through AI systems. Navigation apps reroute us around traffic, smart devices adjust to our preferences, and online services personalize our experiences. We often take these capabilities for granted, yet they represent remarkable advances in artificial intelligence.

The applications we encounter daily build upon the technologies and mechanics explored in previous chapters. Machine learning enables systems to improve their performance over time. Neural networks power pattern recognition in images and speech. Natural language processing facilitates communication between humans and machines. Data, algorithms, and training combine to create tools that enhance our capabilities and simplify our lives.

Consider how AI assists with daily communication. Email systems use machine learning to distinguish spam from legitimate messages, neural networks to recognize patterns in communication, and natural language processing to understand message content. These technologies work together seamlessly, demonstrating how theoretical concepts translate into practical benefits.

Similar integration appears across industries and applications. Healthcare professionals use AI to assist with diagnoses and treatment planning. Financial institutions employ it for fraud detection and risk assessment. Manufacturers utilize it for quality control and production optimization. Each application demonstrates AI's ability to enhance human capabilities and improve operational efficiency.

As we explore these applications in detail, we'll see how AI technologies adapt to different contexts and requirements. Some applications prioritize speed, others accuracy. Some focus on automation, others on augmenting human decision-making. Understanding these variations helps explain both current implementations and future possibilities.

The most direct experience most of us have with artificial intelligence comes through personal technology. These applications demonstrate AI's practical impact while showcasing how sophisticated technologies can become seamlessly integrated into daily life.

Virtual assistants represent one of the most visible applications of AI in personal technology. When you ask Siri, Alexa, or Google Assistant a question, multiple AI technologies work together to understand your request and provide appropriate responses. Natural language processing interprets your words, machine learning helps improve understanding over time, and various specialized systems handle specific types of requests.

These assistants grow more capable through regular use. They learn to recognize your voice more accurately, understand your preferences more clearly, and provide more relevant responses. This practical application of AI learning demonstrates how systems can adapt to individual users while maintaining reliable general functionality.

Email represents another realm where AI quietly improves our daily experience. Modern email systems employ sophisticated AI to help manage the flood of messages most of us receive. Spam filtering provides an excellent example of machine learning in action. These systems continuously learn from new examples of spam and legitimate messages, adapting to evolving threats while minimizing false positives.

Message categorization goes beyond simple spam filtering. AI systems analyze message content and patterns to automatically sort emails into categories like promotions, updates, or personal correspondence. Smart reply features suggest appropriate responses based on message content and your past communications, saving time while maintaining natural interaction.

Perhaps nowhere does AI affect personal choice more directly than in entertainment recommendations. Streaming services analyze viewing patterns to suggest movies and shows. Music platforms create personalized playlists based on listening history. These recommendations combine analysis of content characteristics with patterns of user preference to create increasingly accurate suggestions.

Social media platforms employ similar technology to personalize news feeds and content delivery. AI systems analyze user interaction patterns to determine what content to show, when to show it, and how to maintain user engagement. This personalization demonstrates both the power and the responsibility of AI in shaping personal experience.

Navigation applications showcase AI's ability to process real-time data for immediate practical benefit. These apps analyze traffic patterns, consider multiple route options, and provide updated guidance as conditions change. This real-time processing and adaptation exemplifies how AI can enhance decision-making in dynamic situations.

Calendar management and personal organization tools increasingly incorporate AI to help streamline daily life. These applications learn from your patterns and preferences to suggest meeting times, remind you of important tasks, and help maintain productive schedules. Such applications demonstrate how AI can serve as an intelligent assistant rather than just an automated system.

While personal technology provides our most direct contact with AI, broader industrial applications demonstrate its transformative potential. Across various sectors, artificial intelligence reshapes how organizations operate, serve customers, and solve complex problems.

In healthcare, AI enhances both diagnosis and treatment. Medical imaging systems use advanced pattern recognition to help identify potential issues in X-rays, MRIs, and other diagnostic images. These systems can process images more quickly than human experts while highlighting areas that merit closer examination, enabling more efficient and thorough analysis.

Treatment planning benefits from AI analysis of vast medical databases. Systems can compare patient data with millions of similar cases, helping healthcare providers identify effective treatment options. This capability proves particularly valuable with complex conditions requiring careful consideration of multiple factors and treatment combinations.

The financial sector employs AI extensively for both security and service. Fraud detection systems monitor transactions continuously, identifying suspicious patterns that might indicate criminal activity. These systems learn from each new case of fraud, constantly improving their ability to protect customers while minimizing false alarms.

Investment and trading applications demonstrate AI's capability to process vast amounts of information quickly. AI systems analyze market data, news reports, and economic indicators to identify trading opportunities and assess risks. This processing power enables faster, more informed decision-making in rapidly changing markets.

Retail experiences transformation through AI both online and in physical stores. Online retailers use AI to personalize shopping experiences, recommend products, and optimize inventory management. These systems analyze shopping patterns, predict demand, and help ensure products are available when customers want them.

Physical retail spaces incorporate AI through innovative systems like automated checkouts and smart inventory management. Computer vision systems track product movement, while predictive analytics help stores maintain optimal stock levels. These applications enhance both operational efficiency and customer experience.

Modern manufacturing facilities showcase AI's ability to improve complex operations. Quality control systems use computer vision to identify defects more accurately than human inspection. Predictive maintenance systems monitor equipment performance, identifying potential problems before they cause failures.

Robotics integration demonstrates how AI can complement human capabilities. Smart manufacturing systems coordinate human and robotic workers, optimizing production while maintaining safety and efficiency. These systems continuously learn from operation data, improving processes over time.

Education sees significant transformation through AI-powered learning platforms. These systems can adapt to individual student needs, providing personalized learning experiences at scale. Assessment tools offer immediate feedback, while content delivery systems adjust to each student's pace and learning style.

Language learning applications exemplify this personalization. These systems recognize speech patterns, correct pronunciation, and adjust lesson difficulty based on student performance. This individualized approach helps students learn more effectively while maintaining engagement.

The widespread adoption of AI across personal technology and industry sectors creates significant changes in how we interact, work, and conduct business. Understanding these impacts helps organizations and individuals better prepare for continued technological evolution.

AI reshapes social interactions in fundamental ways. Communication becomes more efficient but also more mediated by technology. Virtual assistants and chatbots handle increasing amounts of routine interaction. While this automation offers convenience, it also changes expectations about personal and professional communication.

Privacy considerations emerge as AI systems collect and process more personal data. The same capabilities that enable personalized experiences also raise questions about data usage and protection. Organizations must balance the benefits of AI-driven personalization with responsible data management and user privacy.

The user experience continues to evolve as AI systems become more sophisticated. People increasingly expect immediate responses, personalized service, and seamless interactions across different platforms and devices. These expectations influence both personal technology development and business service delivery.

Organizations implementing AI systems experience both

opportunities and challenges. Operational efficiency often improves through automation and enhanced decision-making support. Customer service capabilities expand through AI-powered interaction channels. However, successful implementation requires careful planning and consideration of various factors.

Cost considerations play a crucial role in AI adoption. While AI systems can reduce operational costs over time, initial implementation often requires significant investment in technology, training, and process adaptation. Organizations must evaluate potential returns against implementation costs and ongoing maintenance requirements.

The human factor remains crucial in AI implementation. Staff members need training to work effectively with AI systems. Business processes require adjustment to incorporate AI capabilities. Success often depends as much on managing organizational change as on implementing technology.

Implementation challenges vary across different contexts. Some organizations struggle with data quality or availability. Others face integration issues with existing systems. Many encounter resistance to change or difficulty maintaining system performance over time. Understanding these challenges helps organizations prepare more effectively for AI adoption.

Understanding current AI applications provides a foundation for anticipating future developments. As technology continues to evolve, new possibilities emerge while existing applications become more sophisticated and capable.

Several trends suggest future directions for AI applications. Voice interfaces continue to become more natural and context-aware, potentially changing how we interact with technology in fundamental ways. Visual AI systems improve their ability to understand and respond to complex scenes, enabling new applications in areas from autonomous vehicles to medical diagnosis.

The integration of AI with multiple internet-connected

devices creates possibilities for more responsive environments. Smart homes learn occupant preferences and adjust automatically. Manufacturing systems adapt to changing conditions in real time. Healthcare monitoring becomes more continuous and preventive rather than reactive.

Workplace applications show particular promise for development. AI assistants may become more capable of handling complex tasks, from scheduling meetings to drafting documents. Collaborative robots could work more naturally alongside humans in various settings. Training systems might adapt more precisely to individual learning styles and needs.

Organizations considering future AI implementation face several important considerations. Data requirements continue to evolve, with systems needing not just more data but better-quality and more diverse data. Privacy and security concerns require ongoing attention as systems become more sophisticated and interconnected.

Implementation approaches may need to adapt as technology advances. Organizations must consider how to integrate new capabilities while maintaining existing systems. Training requirements evolve as AI systems take on more complex roles. Cost considerations remain important as organizations balance potential benefits against implementation challenges.

The human factor grows increasingly important as AI capabilities expand. Organizations need strategies for helping people work effectively with more sophisticated AI systems. Education and training programs must evolve to prepare workers for changing technological environments. Management approaches need to adapt to new ways of working.

These considerations suggest the importance of flexible, adaptable approaches to AI implementation. Organizations that maintain awareness of emerging possibilities while carefully considering practical implementation factors will be better positioned to take advantage of new opportunities as they arise.

As we conclude our exploration of AI in everyday life, we find ourselves at an interesting intersection of current capability and future potential. The applications we've examined demonstrate both the remarkable progress already achieved and the significant developments still to come.

Current AI applications will likely become more sophisticated and capable. Personal assistants may develop deeper understanding of context and user preferences. Healthcare systems could provide more comprehensive and personalized analysis. Manufacturing applications might achieve new levels of efficiency and adaptation.

The integration of AI into daily life will probably become even more seamless. Rather than interacting with distinct AI applications, we may find ourselves in environments where AI support feels natural and continuous. This evolution suggests not just technological advancement but changes in how we think about and interact with artificial intelligence.

The boundary between AI and human capabilities continues to shift. While some tasks become increasingly automated, human judgment and creativity remain crucial. Understanding this relationship helps prepare for future developments while maintaining perspective about both capabilities and limitations.

Organizations and individuals can prepare for continued AI evolution in several ways. Maintaining awareness of technological developments helps identify new opportunities. Understanding implementation challenges enables better planning. Considering human factors ensures more effective integration of new capabilities.

Education and training take on increasing importance as AI applications evolve. Technical understanding helps people work effectively with AI systems. Awareness of capabilities and limitations supports better decision-making about AI implementation. Recognition of human factors contributes to successful integration.

The pace of AI development suggests the importance of maintaining flexibility in approaches to implementation and use. Rather than seeking fixed solutions, organizations and individuals benefit from developing adaptable strategies that can evolve alongside technological capabilities.

As we look toward future chapters exploring more specific aspects of AI development and implementation, this understanding of practical applications provides valuable context. It helps us appreciate both the current impact of artificial intelligence and its potential for continued transformation of how we live and work.

While these applications demonstrate remarkable capabilities, they also reveal important boundaries and constraints in AI operation. Understanding these limitations proves just as crucial as appreciating AI's potential. In our next chapter, we'll examine the practical constraints and operational boundaries that shape how AI systems function in real-world applications.

CHAPTER 8: AI LIMITATIONS AND CONSTRAINTS

Our exploration of artificial intelligence thus far has revealed remarkable capabilities across various applications. However, understanding AI's limitations and constraints proves just as crucial as appreciating its potential. These boundaries shape not just how AI systems operate, but how we should approach their implementation and use.

While artificial intelligence continues advancing rapidly, it operates within specific constraints that affect its capabilities and reliability. Understanding these limitations helps establish realistic expectations and ensure appropriate implementation. This knowledge proves particularly crucial as AI systems take on more significant roles in various aspects of life and business.

Many limitations stem from fundamental aspects of how AI systems work. Unlike human intelligence, which can readily adapt to new situations and transfer knowledge between domains, AI operates within boundaries defined by its training and design. Even the most sophisticated AI remains fundamentally a pattern recognition and prediction system, lacking true understanding or consciousness.

AI systems face various types of limitations, from fundamental constraints in their operation to practical challenges in implementation. Technical limitations involve computational resources, storage capacity, and processing capabilities. Operational constraints affect how systems maintain context and handle extended interactions. Understanding these different types of constraints helps guide effective AI utilization.

Some limitations arise from the nature of artificial intelligence itself. Language models can produce "hallucinations," generating plausible but incorrect information with high confidence. Systems may struggle with common-sense reasoning that humans perform naturally. These inherent limitations require specific consideration in AI application.

The practical impact of AI limitations affects how organizations implement and use these systems. Resource constraints might require specific measures for managing system load and performance. Storage limitations could affect how systems maintain context during interactions. Processing constraints might influence how complex tasks are structured and executed.

Understanding these impacts helps organizations plan more effectively for AI implementation. Rather than expecting unlimited capability, they can design systems and processes that work within known constraints while maximizing available capabilities. This realistic approach leads to more successful AI deployment and utilization.

At its core, artificial intelligence operates through pattern recognition, a characteristic that creates inherent limitations. Unlike human intelligence, which can truly understand and reason about new situations, AI systems recognize and respond to patterns in their training data. This fundamental nature restricts how these systems can handle novel or unexpected situations.

When encountering scenarios that differ significantly from their training data, AI systems may fail to perform effectively. A system trained to recognize cats in photographs might struggle with drawings or unusual perspectives. This limitation extends across all AI applications, from image recognition to decision-making systems.

Training data itself creates boundaries for AI capability. Systems can only learn from the data they're trained on, making them inherently limited by the scope and quality of that data. While they might perform impressively within their trained domains, they lack the human ability to readily adapt knowledge to new contexts.

One of the most significant limitations in current AI systems appears in language models' tendency to generate false information with high confidence. These "hallucinations" occur when systems construct plausible-sounding but incorrect responses based on patterns in their training data rather than true understanding.

Consider how a language model might describe historical events. While usually accurate when the information clearly exists in its training data, it might confidently combine or confuse details, creating convincing but inaccurate descriptions. This tendency makes human verification crucial for factual accuracy.

The challenge of hallucinations proves particularly important because these systems often express incorrect information with the same confidence as accurate information. Users might find it difficult to distinguish between reliable responses and hallucinations without external verification.

AI systems fundamentally lack true understanding of the information they process. While they can identify patterns and generate appropriate responses, they don't comprehend meaning in the way humans do. This limitation affects their ability to handle context, nuance, and implied meaning.

The absence of common sense reasoning creates particular challenges. Tasks that humans handle intuitively through general knowledge and logical reasoning might prove difficult for AI systems lacking this fundamental understanding. Simple contextual shifts that humans navigate easily can cause AI systems to produce inappropriate or incorrect responses.

These limitations in understanding and context affect how AI systems maintain coherence in extended interactions. While they might perform well in structured, well-defined scenarios, they can struggle when situations require broader understanding or contextual adaptation.

AI systems require substantial computational power to function effectively, creating practical limitations on their operation. Large language models, for instance, need significant processing capacity to analyze inputs and generate responses. These resource requirements directly affect system performance and capability.

Memory constraints particularly impact how AI systems handle complex or lengthy tasks. Extended conversations or complex analyses might face limitations due to memory capacity. These constraints can force systems to truncate interactions or break complex tasks into smaller segments, affecting their practical utility.

The relationship between model sophistication and computational demands creates additional challenges. More advanced AI capabilities typically require greater computational resources. Organizations must balance desired functionality against available processing power, often leading to practical compromises in system implementation.

While AI systems can process vast amounts of data, they face significant constraints in data storage and retention. These limitations manifest not just in how systems maintain context during interactions, but also in practical usage constraints. Many AI services must implement specific limits on how much data users can process within given time periods to manage system resources effectively.

Session data presents particular challenges. Systems often cannot maintain indefinite conversation histories or accumulate knowledge through ongoing interactions. Each session typically starts fresh, without retained context from previous interactions. This limitation affects how systems maintain consistency and context in extended engagements.

The challenge extends beyond simple storage capacity to include data access and management. Quick access to relevant information requires careful balance between storage capacity and retrieval speed. These technical constraints influence both system design and practical implementation, often requiring specific measures to manage user access and system resources.

Resource demands create various performance constraints in AI systems. Processing delays might occur during complex operations or high-usage periods. System timeouts might interrupt extended interactions to free resources for other users. These performance limitations affect how users can interact with AI systems effectively.

Load management presents ongoing challenges. Systems must balance multiple users and tasks while maintaining acceptable performance levels. This balancing act often requires compromises between system availability and individual session capabilities.

The interaction between different resource constraints, processing power, memory, storage, and network capacity, creates complex performance challenges. Organizations must manage these various constraints while maintaining system effectiveness and user satisfaction.

The practical operation of AI systems requires careful management of user sessions and interactions. Systems must maintain appropriate boundaries for individual sessions while ensuring fair resource allocation across multiple users. These operational requirements create specific limitations on how users can interact with AI systems.

Session constraints affect various aspects of system operation. Extended interactions might require breaking into multiple sessions to manage resource usage effectively. Complex tasks might need restructuring to work within session limitations. These boundaries shape how organizations can implement AI systems for practical applications.

Effective session management often requires specific protocols for handling interruptions or transitions between sessions. Users and organizations must understand these operational boundaries to design effective workflows and processes around AI system capabilities.

AI systems face various constraints in how they process and handle data during operations. Input limitations might restrict the size or complexity of queries and requests. Processing capacity affects how quickly systems can analyze and respond to complex tasks. Output generation might face constraints based on system resources and capabilities.

The relationship between data complexity and processing requirements creates practical operational boundaries. More complex data typically requires more processing resources and time. Organizations must consider these relationships when designing AI implementations and setting expectations for system performance.

Data quality and format requirements create additional operational considerations. Systems might have specific limitations on acceptable data types or structures. These requirements affect how organizations prepare and present data for AI processing.

AI systems, like any complex technology, face reliability challenges that affect their operational consistency. Performance may vary based on system load, data characteristics, or other factors. Understanding these reliability constraints helps organizations plan for effective system implementation.

Dependency factors create additional operational considerations. Systems might rely on various external resources or services, each with its own limitations and constraints. These dependencies can affect overall system reliability and performance.

Managing system reliability requires understanding both typical performance patterns and potential variation factors. Organizations need appropriate protocols for handling performance fluctuations and maintaining consistent service levels within operational boundaries.

Implementing AI systems requires careful management of available resources to maintain effective operation. Organizations must balance system capabilities against resource constraints while ensuring consistent performance. This balancing act often involves complex decisions about resource allocation and system optimization.

Load balancing presents particular challenges in AI implementation. Systems must handle varying user demands while maintaining performance standards. Organizations often need specific strategies for managing peak usage periods and distributing system load effectively.

Performance tuning requires ongoing attention to system operation and resource utilization. Organizations must monitor system performance, adjust resource allocation, and optimize operations based on actual usage patterns. These requirements create continuous management challenges in AI implementation.

Real-world implementation of AI systems reveals various practical challenges beyond technical constraints. Integration with existing systems might face compatibility limitations or resource conflicts. Organizations must consider how AI systems will work within their current technological environment.

Scaling presents significant challenges in AI implementation. As usage grows, resource requirements typically increase accordingly. Organizations must plan for growth while managing current operational needs. This balance affects both system design and implementation strategy.

Cost considerations often influence implementation decisions. Resource requirements, system maintenance, and operational support all contribute to implementation expenses. Organizations must balance desired capabilities against practical budget constraints.

The deployment of AI systems depends heavily on supporting infrastructure. Network capacity, storage systems, and processing resources must meet system requirements while allowing for potential growth. These infrastructure needs create specific implementation challenges.

Many organizations face limitations in available infrastructure. Upgrading or expanding infrastructure to support AI systems might require significant investment. These constraints affect how organizations can implement and utilize AI capabilities.

Infrastructure reliability also impacts system implementation. Organizations need redundancy and backup capabilities to maintain system operation. These requirements add complexity to AI system implementation while affecting overall system reliability.

Despite their sophisticated capabilities, AI systems require consistent human oversight to ensure accurate and appropriate operation. This necessity for oversight stems from fundamental limitations in AI capabilities, particularly the potential for errors or inappropriate responses.

Verification of AI outputs becomes crucial in many applications. Users must validate system responses, particularly for critical decisions or factual information. This verification requirement creates an ongoing need for human involvement in AI operations, even in highly automated systems.

Quality control processes need human judgment to maintain appropriate standards. Organizations must establish specific protocols for reviewing AI system performance and outputs. These oversight requirements affect how organizations can implement and utilize AI capabilities effectively.

The effectiveness of AI systems often depends heavily on how humans interact with them. Clear, well-structured inputs typically produce better results than vague or ambiguous requests. This relationship between input quality and system performance creates specific requirements for user interaction.

Proper prompting has emerged as a crucial skill for effective AI utilization. Users need understanding of how to frame requests and queries to obtain optimal results. This requirement for skilled interaction affects how organizations can implement AI systems and who can effectively use them.

Result interpretation also requires human judgment and expertise. Users must understand both system capabilities and limitations to properly evaluate outputs. This need for informed interpretation creates ongoing requirements for user training and support.

Organizations implementing AI systems must invest in human capacity development. Users need training in system capabilities, limitations, and proper interaction methods. This training requirement extends beyond technical skills to include understanding of AI limitations and appropriate use cases.

Adapting organizational processes to work effectively with AI systems requires careful attention to human factors. Workflows must account for both system capabilities and human oversight requirements. This adaptation process affects how organizations can effectively implement and utilize AI systems.

The ongoing evolution of AI capabilities requires continuous learning and adaptation from users and organizations. As systems advance, interaction methods and oversight requirements may change. This dynamic creates continuing needs for training and process adaptation.

The limitations and constraints we've examined represent current realities in artificial intelligence systems. Understanding these boundaries helps set appropriate expectations while enabling effective system implementation.

As technology advances, some constraints may shift or change, but fundamental limitations are likely to persist.

Many current limitations stem from basic aspects of how AI systems work. The need for extensive computational resources, storage capacity, and processing power creates practical constraints that affect system operation. While technology continues advancing, managing these resource requirements remains a crucial consideration.

The challenge of AI limitations extends beyond technical constraints to include fundamental aspects of system capability. Issues like language model hallucinations, context maintenance, and the need for human oversight represent more than temporary technical challenges. These limitations reflect current understanding of artificial intelligence and its capabilities.

As AI technology continues evolving, organizations must prepare for changing limitations and constraints. New capabilities might address some current limitations while potentially introducing new ones. Understanding this dynamic helps organizations plan for future AI implementation and use.

Resource management will likely remain a crucial consideration even as technology advances. Organizations must continue balancing system capabilities against available resources while maintaining effective operation. This balance between capability and constraint will shape how AI systems develop and deploy.

The role of human oversight and interaction in AI systems will continue evolving. While some current limitations might ease with technological advancement, the need for human judgment and verification likely remains important. Organizations must prepare for ongoing adaptation in how humans and AI systems work together.

Looking ahead, successful AI implementation requires understanding both capabilities and constraints. Organizations that recognize and plan for these limitations while maintaining realistic expectations will likely achieve more effective results. This balanced approach helps ensure artificial intelligence serves as a valuable tool while acknowledging its inherent boundaries.

GIL OREN

CHAPTER 9: ETHICAL CHALLENGES IN AI

As artificial intelligence becomes increasingly integrated into our lives and society, we face crucial questions about its ethical implications. The remarkable capabilities we've explored in previous chapters bring not just technological opportunities but also significant moral and social responsibilities.

The power of artificial intelligence to influence decisions, shape experiences, and affect lives demands careful ethical consideration. When AI systems determine who gets a loan, who receives particular medical treatments, or who gets called for job interviews, their impact extends far beyond technical performance into questions of fairness, transparency, and social justice.

Consider how AI systems make decisions. Unlike human decision-makers who can explain their reasoning and be held accountable for their choices, AI systems often operate as "black boxes," making choices based on patterns in data that may be difficult to understand or explain. This opacity raises fundamental questions about responsibility and accountability.

The speed and scale at which AI systems operate amplify these ethical concerns. A biased human decision affects one interaction at a time. A biased AI system can affect thousands or millions of decisions rapidly and simultaneously. This multiplication of impact makes addressing ethical considerations not just important but crucial for responsible AI development.

Approaching ethical challenges in AI requires considering multiple perspectives and balancing various interests. Technical capability must be weighed against social responsibility. Efficiency and automation must be balanced against fairness and human dignity. Innovation must proceed with careful consideration of potential consequences.

Several key areas demand particular attention. Bias in AI systems can perpetuate or amplify existing social inequalities. Privacy concerns arise as AI systems collect and process increasing amounts of personal data. Questions of accountability emerge when AI systems make important decisions. The potential for job displacement raises broader societal concerns.

These challenges require more than technical solutions. They demand careful consideration of values, principles, and social impact. As we develop and deploy AI systems, we must consider not just what technology can do, but what it should do and how it should be governed.

The ethical considerations we explore in this chapter will help frame both current challenges and future developments in artificial intelligence. Understanding these issues proves essential for anyone involved in developing, implementing, or using AI systems.

As we examine specific ethical challenges, we'll see how they interconnect and influence each other. We'll also explore how addressing these challenges requires ongoing dialogue between technologists, ethicists, policymakers, and the broader public.

Among the ethical challenges facing artificial intelligence, bias stands out as particularly crucial. AI systems, designed to learn from data and make decisions, can inadvertently perpetuate or amplify existing societal biases. Understanding this challenge proves essential for developing and implementing AI responsibly.

Bias in AI systems often begins with training data. When systems learn from historical data, they can inherit past prejudices and discriminatory patterns. For instance, if an AI system learns from historical hiring data where certain groups were underrepresented, it might perpetuate these same patterns in its recommendations.

This issue becomes particularly significant because AI systems can give these historical biases a veneer of technological objectivity. People might assume that because a computer made a decision, it must be free from human prejudice. In reality, AI systems can encode and amplify human biases through their training data and algorithmic decisions.

The problem extends beyond obvious forms of discrimination. Subtle biases can emerge in unexpected ways. A facial recognition system trained primarily on certain demographic groups might perform poorly on others. A medical diagnostic system trained mainly on data from one population might make less accurate predictions for others.

The impact of AI bias appears across numerous domains. In hiring processes, AI systems screening resumes might favor candidates from particular backgrounds based on historical patterns rather than actual qualifications. Financial services using AI for credit decisions might perpetuate existing economic disparities by relying on data that reflects past discrimination.

Healthcare provides particularly concerning examples. AI systems analyzing medical images or recommending treatments might perform differently for different demographic groups based on imbalances in their training data. These disparities can have serious consequences for patient care and outcomes.

Law enforcement applications raise additional concerns. Facial recognition systems with varying accuracy rates across different populations can lead to discriminatory outcomes. Predictive policing systems might reinforce existing patterns of over-policing in certain communities.

The business impact of bias extends beyond ethical concerns to practical considerations. AI systems that exhibit bias can damage company reputations, expose organizations to legal liability, and alienate customers or employees. Addressing bias becomes both a moral imperative and a business necessity.

Recognizing these implications helps drive efforts to address bias in AI systems. Technical solutions include improving data collection to ensure better representation, developing algorithms that can detect and correct for bias, and implementing rigorous testing procedures across different populations.

However, technical solutions alone prove insufficient. Addressing AI bias requires broader consideration of social context, careful attention to system design and implementation, and ongoing monitoring of outcomes. It demands collaboration between technologists, domain experts, and affected communities.

The power of artificial intelligence systems depends heavily on their access to data. This fundamental requirement creates significant privacy challenges as organizations collect, store, and process increasingly personal information. Understanding these privacy implications becomes crucial for responsible AI development and deployment.

Modern AI systems collect vast amounts of personal data, often in ways users might not fully understand. Smart devices record our conversations, apps track our locations, and online services monitor our behaviors. While this data enables personalized services and improved functionality, it also raises serious privacy considerations.

AI BASICS: THE FUNDAMENTALS

Consider how a virtual assistant works. To provide personalized responses, it must process voice commands, understand user preferences, and often access personal information like calendars or contacts. Each interaction adds to a growing collection of personal data that could reveal significant details about an individual's life, habits, and relationships.

The scope of data collection extends far beyond obvious interactions. AI systems might analyze shopping patterns, monitor health indicators through wearable devices, or track professional activities through productivity tools. This comprehensive data collection creates detailed profiles of individual behavior and preferences.

The storage and protection of collected data presents its own challenges. Organizations must safeguard vast amounts of personal information from unauthorized access while maintaining its availability for legitimate use. Data breaches can expose sensitive personal information, leading to significant harm for individuals and organizations alike.

Privacy concerns become particularly acute when different data sources combine. Individual pieces of information might seem innocuous, but when analyzed together through AI systems, they can reveal surprisingly detailed insights about personal lives. This capability for deep analysis makes privacy protection increasingly challenging.

Surveillance and monitoring capabilities raise additional concerns. AI-powered systems can track individuals across physical and digital spaces, analyze behavior patterns, and make predictions about future actions. These capabilities, while valuable for security and service delivery, also create potential for privacy invasion and misuse.

The global nature of data collection and AI deployment complicates privacy protection further. Different regions have varying privacy regulations and expectations. Organizations must navigate complex legal requirements while managing data across international boundaries.

Technical solutions like encryption and anonymization help address some privacy concerns. However, the effectiveness of these measures faces ongoing challenges as AI systems become more sophisticated at analyzing and correlating data. Privacy protection requires continuous adaptation to emerging capabilities and threats.

Beyond technical measures, organizations must consider ethical implications of data collection and use. This includes being transparent about data practices, obtaining proper consent, and providing users with control over their personal information. Balancing the benefits of AI capabilities with privacy protection remains an ongoing challenge.

As artificial intelligence systems make increasingly significant decisions affecting people's lives, questions of accountability and responsibility become paramount. When AI systems influence medical treatments, financial opportunities, or legal outcomes, understanding who bears responsibility for these decisions takes on critical importance.

When an AI system makes a decision, determining responsibility proves more complex than with traditional human decisions. If an AI system denies a loan application or recommends against a medical treatment, who bears responsibility for that choice? The software developers, the organization deploying the system, or some combination of parties may all share accountability.

Medical diagnosis provides a clear example of these challenges. If an AI system misses a crucial diagnosis that a human doctor might have caught, who bears responsibility? Conversely, if a doctor follows an AI system's recommendation that leads to adverse outcomes, how should responsibility be allocated between the human decision-maker and the AI system?

The complexity increases when systems make automated decisions at scale. A single flawed decision logic can affect thousands of individuals simultaneously. This multiplication of impact makes clear accountability frameworks even more crucial while often making them more difficult to establish.

Addressing accountability requires transparency in how AI systems make decisions. Users, whether professionals relying on AI recommendations or individuals affected by AI decisions, need to understand the basis for these choices. This transparency enables meaningful human oversight and appropriate attribution of responsibility.

However, achieving transparency presents significant challenges. Many modern AI systems, particularly deep learning models, operate as "black boxes" where the path to a decision may not be easily explained. This opacity complicates efforts to assess responsibility when outcomes prove problematic.

Organizations implementing AI systems must develop frameworks for monitoring and explaining system decisions. This includes establishing clear chains of responsibility, implementing audit procedures, and creating mechanisms for addressing concerns or challenging decisions. Without such frameworks, accountability remains difficult to maintain.

Legal and regulatory requirements increasingly demand explicability in AI decision-making. Organizations must demonstrate that their AI systems make decisions fairly and transparently, particularly in regulated industries like healthcare and finance. Meeting these requirements while maintaining system effectiveness presents ongoing challenges.

The human role in AI decision-making requires particular attention. While AI systems can process vast amounts of data and identify patterns humans might miss, human judgment often proves crucial for contextualizing and validating AI recommendations. Establishing appropriate human oversight while maintaining efficient operations presents another key challenge.

The ethical implications of artificial intelligence extend beyond individual privacy and fairness to broader societal concerns. As AI systems become more prevalent, their collective impact on employment, social structures, and human interaction requires careful consideration.

Perhaps no societal impact generates more discussion than AI's effect on employment. While artificial intelligence creates new jobs in technology and related fields, it also automates tasks traditionally performed by humans. This transformation affects not just individual jobs but entire industries and economic structures.

Consider customer service roles, where AI chatbots and virtual assistants increasingly handle routine inquiries. While this automation improves efficiency and availability, it also changes employment patterns in the industry. Similar transitions occur in manufacturing, data analysis, and even professional services where AI systems take on more complex tasks.

The impact varies across different segments of society. Some workers find opportunities to transition to new roles working with AI systems. Others face challenges as their skills become less relevant in an AI-enhanced workplace. This disparity in impact raises important questions about societal responsibility for managing this transition.

Beyond employment, AI influences how people interact and communicate. Social media algorithms shape what information we see and how we connect with others. Recommendation systems influence our choices in entertainment, shopping, and even relationships. These influences raise questions about autonomy and authentic human interaction.

The automation of services affects community structures as well. As more interactions occur through AI-mediated channels, traditional social bonds and community connections may weaken. The convenience of AI-powered services might come at the cost of human connection and social cohesion.

Educational systems face particular challenges as AI transforms both learning environments and future career preparation. Schools must balance teaching traditional skills with preparing students for an AI-enhanced workplace. This includes not just technical knowledge but also uniquely human capabilities that complement AI systems.

Cultural implications emerge as AI systems interact with different social norms and values. Systems designed with one cultural context in mind might not translate well to others. This raises questions about preserving cultural diversity while developing globally applicable AI solutions.

The concentration of AI development within certain companies and regions creates additional societal concerns. Questions of power, influence, and access to technology become increasingly important as AI systems affect more aspects of daily life. Ensuring equitable access to AI benefits while protecting against negative impacts presents ongoing challenges.

The ethical challenges we've explored require structured approaches for addressing them. Building effective ethical frameworks helps organizations develop and deploy AI systems responsibly while maintaining innovation and progress.

Effective ethical frameworks begin with clear principles that guide AI development and deployment. These principles might include fairness in system outcomes, transparency in decision-making processes, respect for privacy, and commitment to human welfare. Such principles provide foundation for more specific guidelines and practices.

For example, a principle of fairness leads to specific requirements for testing AI systems across different populations. Privacy principles translate into detailed data protection protocols. Transparency commitments result in requirements for explaining system decisions. These practical implementations help transform abstract principles into concrete actions.

Organizations must also consider how different principles interact and sometimes conflict. Maximizing system accuracy might require more data collection, potentially conflicting with privacy protection. Ensuring human oversight might reduce efficiency. Resolving such conflicts requires careful balancing of competing priorities.

Moving from principles to practice requires specific processes and procedures. Organizations need clear guidelines for data collection and use, testing protocols for identifying bias, and procedures for monitoring system performance. These practical measures help ensure ethical principles translate into daily operations.

Implementation also requires appropriate organizational structures. This might include ethics review boards for new AI applications, regular audits of system performance, and clear channels for raising and addressing concerns. Such structures help embed ethical considerations into organizational culture and decision-making.

Training plays a crucial role in implementation success. Technical teams need understanding of ethical implications in their work. Management needs awareness of ethical considerations in strategic decisions. Users need knowledge of system capabilities and limitations. This comprehensive training helps create shared responsibility for ethical AI development.

Continuous monitoring and adjustment prove essential as AI systems evolve. Regular review of system performance, impact assessments, and updates to ethical guidelines help organizations maintain responsible practices while adapting to new challenges and capabilities.

Industry collaboration can strengthen ethical frameworks. Sharing best practices, developing common standards, and addressing shared challenges collectively helps advance ethical AI development across the field. This collaboration becomes particularly important as AI systems increasingly interact across organizational boundaries.

The ethical challenges facing artificial intelligence continue to evolve as technology advances and societal understanding deepens. Looking ahead helps us prepare for emerging challenges while building on current insights and frameworks.

AI BASICS: THE FUNDAMENTALS

As AI systems become more sophisticated, new ethical considerations will likely emerge. Advanced language models raise questions about authenticity and truth in communication. Increasingly autonomous systems challenge existing frameworks for responsibility and control. More powerful prediction capabilities create new privacy and fairness concerns.

The integration of AI into critical infrastructure and essential services demands increasingly robust ethical frameworks. Healthcare, transportation, financial systems, and public safety applications require careful consideration of both current and potential future impacts. Preparing for these developments requires forward-thinking approaches to ethical guidelines.

International cooperation becomes increasingly important as AI systems cross borders and affect global communities. Different cultural perspectives on privacy, fairness, and accountability need consideration. Developing ethical frameworks that work across diverse contexts while respecting local values presents ongoing challenges.

The path forward requires balancing technological progress with ethical considerations. Innovation must continue while maintaining responsible development practices. This balance becomes particularly important as competition in AI development intensifies globally.

Education and public discourse play crucial roles in shaping future developments. Technical professionals need deeper understanding of ethical implications. The public needs better awareness of both AI capabilities and limitations. Policymakers need informed perspectives on regulatory needs and approaches.

Organizations developing and deploying AI systems must maintain focus on both short-term and long-term ethical considerations. While addressing immediate concerns, they must also prepare for emerging challenges. This dual focus helps ensure sustainable and responsible AI development.

The ethical challenges we've explored in this chapter will likely remain relevant even as new ones emerge. Bias, privacy, accountability, and societal impact continue requiring attention while novel challenges arise. Understanding these foundational issues helps prepare for future developments.

As we move forward to explore more specific aspects of AI development and implementation in coming chapters, these ethical considerations provide crucial context. They remind us that technological capability must align with human values and societal benefit for truly successful AI development.

CHAPTER 10: UNPACKING AI BIAS

In our exploration of ethical challenges in artificial intelligence, bias emerged as a critical concern. Now we must examine this issue more deeply, understanding how AI systems can inadvertently perpetuate and sometimes amplify societal prejudices and inequalities.

Bias in artificial intelligence differs from human prejudice in important ways. While human bias often stems from personal experiences, beliefs, or conscious preferences, AI bias typically emerges from data patterns and system design choices. This distinction proves crucial for understanding both how bias develops in AI systems and how we might address it.

Consider how an AI system learns. It processes vast amounts of data, identifying patterns and relationships that inform its decisions. If this data reflects historical inequalities or societal prejudices, the system may learn to replicate these biases in its operations. What appears as neutral pattern recognition can actually perpetuate unfair treatment of certain groups or individuals.

The impact of AI bias extends far beyond technical considerations. When AI systems make biased decisions about loans, jobs, medical treatment, or legal matters, they affect people's lives in profound and lasting ways. Understanding AI bias becomes not just a technical challenge but a crucial social responsibility.

AI bias manifests in various forms, each requiring specific recognition and mitigation approaches. Historical bias emerges when systems learn from data that reflects past discriminatory practices. Sampling bias occurs when training data fails to represent all relevant groups adequately. Label bias appears when human prejudices influence how training data is categorized.

The complexity of addressing these biases stems partly from their subtle nature. Unlike obvious forms of discrimination, AI bias often hides within seemingly objective systems. A hiring algorithm might appear to make decisions based purely on qualifications while unknowingly favoring certain demographic groups. A medical diagnostic system might perform less accurately for populations underrepresented in its training data.

Understanding the scope of AI bias requires examining both individual instances and systemic patterns. While individual cases might show clear examples of unfair treatment, the broader impact of AI bias appears in patterns of systemic disadvantage across different applications and contexts.

This challenge grows more significant as AI systems take on increasingly important roles in society. As these systems influence more decisions affecting people's lives, ensuring fairness and preventing bias becomes increasingly crucial. The widespread deployment of AI systems means that biased decisions can affect large populations quickly and simultaneously.

To effectively address bias in artificial intelligence systems, we must first understand its origins. AI bias stems from multiple sources, each contributing to potential unfairness in system outcomes.

When AI systems learn from historical data, they can inherit and perpetuate past prejudices. Consider an AI system analyzing employment records to assist with hiring decisions. If trained on data from an era or industry where women rarely held leadership positions, the system might learn to associate leadership roles primarily with male candidates.

This historical bias extends beyond obvious discrimination. Subtle patterns of past inequality become embedded in data used to train AI systems. Medical records might reflect historical disparities in healthcare access. Lending data might capture past discriminatory practices in financial services. Educational data might mirror systemic inequalities in academic opportunities.

The challenge with historical bias lies in its pervasive nature. Even when obviously discriminatory practices end, their effects persist in historical data. AI systems learning from this data can unknowingly preserve and propagate these past inequities into future decisions.

Sampling bias occurs when training data fails to represent all relevant groups adequately. This often happens unintentionally but can lead to significant disparities in system performance. A facial recognition system trained primarily on one demographic group may perform poorly when attempting to identify members of other groups.

The impact of sampling bias appears particularly in applications requiring broad demographic representation. Healthcare diagnostic systems might perform less accurately for underrepresented populations. Speech recognition systems might struggle with certain accents or dialects. Language processing systems might handle some languages or cultural expressions better than others.

Technology development practices can inadvertently contribute to sampling bias. If development teams lack diversity, they might not recognize gaps in their training data.

Limited data collection resources might lead to overreliance on easily accessible but unrepresentative samples. Cost considerations might restrict efforts to gather more diverse data.

The process of preparing data for AI training can introduce additional bias through labeling and annotation choices. Human annotators bring their own cultural perspectives and potential biases when categorizing training data. These choices influence how AI systems learn to classify and respond to new information.

Language provides clear examples of labeling bias. Decisions about what constitutes "professional" language might reflect cultural biases. Classifications of sentiment or tone might vary across cultural contexts. Judgments about content appropriateness might embed particular cultural values.

Even technical classifications can reflect underlying biases. Choices about how to categorize medical symptoms might reflect experiences with certain populations more than others. Decisions about relevant features in financial data might encode assumptions about economic behavior. Classifications of "normal" versus "suspicious" activity might incorporate stereotypical thinking.

Understanding AI bias moves from theoretical to urgent when we examine its real-world impact. Across various domains, biased AI systems affect crucial decisions and opportunities in people's lives.

AI bias manifests prominently in employment-related applications. Resume screening systems, increasingly common in hiring processes, can disadvantage qualified candidates based on factors unrelated to job performance. These systems might penalize gaps in employment history, potentially discriminating against parents who took career breaks or workers who faced economic disruptions.

Promotion and advancement systems using AI to identify potential leaders might perpetuate existing workplace disparities. If trained on historical patterns of advancement, these systems might overlook qualified candidates from underrepresented groups. Performance evaluation systems might interpret work styles or communication patterns differently across cultural or gender lines.

Facial recognition technology demonstrates some of the most visible examples of AI bias in public services. Systems showing lower accuracy rates for certain demographic groups create serious concerns, particularly in law enforcement applications. Misidentification in security systems can lead to wrongful suspicion, unwarranted stops, or false arrests.

Beyond law enforcement, biased AI systems can affect access to government services and benefits. Automated decision systems determining eligibility for public assistance, housing, or educational opportunities might inadvertently discriminate against certain communities. When these systems fail to account for diverse circumstances or needs, they can reinforce existing social inequities.

In healthcare, AI bias can directly affect patient outcomes. Diagnostic systems trained primarily on data from certain populations might miss or misinterpret symptoms in others. This becomes particularly critical in areas like cancer detection, where early diagnosis significantly impacts survival rates.

Treatment recommendation systems might suggest different approaches based on incomplete or biased data about treatment effectiveness across populations. If clinical trials historically underrepresented certain groups, AI systems learning from this data might make suboptimal recommendations for these populations.

Healthcare access systems using AI to manage appointments, resources, or insurance approvals might inadvertently create disparities in care availability. Geographic or demographic patterns in historical healthcare data might lead to biased assumptions about medical needs or resource allocation.

Identifying bias in AI systems requires systematic

approaches and rigorous testing. Organizations must implement comprehensive methods to detect potential bias before it affects real-world decisions.

Effective bias detection begins with thorough testing protocols. This involves evaluating system performance across different demographic groups and contexts. Testing must go beyond overall accuracy metrics to examine how systems perform for specific populations and situations.

Consider a lending decision system. Testing should examine approval rates across different demographic groups while controlling for relevant financial factors. Disparities in approval rates might indicate potential bias even when the system appears accurate overall. Similar approaches apply to other domains where AI systems make important decisions.

Performance metrics must consider multiple dimensions of fairness. Statistical parity examines whether different groups receive similar outcomes. Individual fairness looks at whether similar individuals receive similar treatment. Equality of opportunity considers whether qualified candidates have similar chances regardless of group membership.

Regular auditing provides structured approaches to examining AI systems for potential bias. These audits should occur throughout system development and deployment, not just during initial testing. Continuous monitoring helps identify emerging bias as systems process new data and encounter new situations.

Thorough audits must examine multiple aspects of system performance. Organizations need to analyze their data to verify representative samples while evaluating algorithms for processing fairness. Outcome assessment becomes crucial for examining decision patterns, as does impact review for considering broader consequences of system decisions.

The establishment of clear procedures proves essential for conducting effective audits. Organizations must determine what constitutes concerning disparities and establish appropriate frequency for reviews. Clear assignment of responsibility for reviews ensures accountability, while defined response procedures guide actions when concerns arise.

Documentation plays a vital role throughout the audit process. Organizations should maintain detailed records of their testing procedures and results, tracking identified concerns and responses over time. System adjustments must be documented, along with their outcomes and ongoing monitoring results. This comprehensive documentation helps organizations track progress and demonstrate their commitment to addressing bias.

Once organizations identify bias in AI systems, they must take concrete steps to address it. Effective mitigation requires comprehensive strategies that address bias at multiple levels, from data collection through system deployment.

Improving training data provides a fundamental approach to reducing AI bias. Organizations must ensure their training datasets represent diverse populations and experiences. This involves not just collecting more data but collecting the right data from appropriate sources.

Quality improvement in training data requires attention to several critical factors. Organizations need to examine demographic representation in their datasets, ensuring proper balance across different groups. The historical context of data sources must be understood and considered, while cultural perspectives in data collection need careful attention.

Collecting truly representative data often requires targeted efforts. Organizations might need to build partnerships with diverse communities to access more varied data sources. Expanding data collection methods helps capture a broader range of experiences and perspectives. Regular validation of data quality across different groups ensures maintained representation, while specific efforts to address historical data gaps help correct past imbalances.

Algorithm adjustments offer another crucial path for bias mitigation. Technical solutions might include developing weighted sampling techniques to balance representation in processing. Organizations can implement bias correction algorithms to adjust for known disparities. Enhanced validation methods help catch potential issues early, while improved testing protocols ensure thorough evaluation of system performance across different groups.

Model improvements focus on how systems process and learn from data. Organizations can implement fairness constraints in their training processes to guide system development. Careful attention to feature selection helps ensure balanced consideration of different factors. Robust validation methods confirm system performance across various scenarios, while regular monitoring tracks ongoing effectiveness.

Technical solutions alone cannot fully address AI bias. Human oversight plays a crucial role in ensuring fair outcomes. Organizations must establish clear processes for regular system review and decision validation. Performance assessment and impact evaluation work together as complementary processes: ongoing monitoring tracks immediate outcomes, while systematic evaluation reveals how system decisions affect both short-term performance and long-term organizational goals.

Effective oversight requires appropriate expertise and authority. Organizations should invest in proper training for their reviewers, establishing clear guidelines for their work. Adequate resources must support oversight efforts, while meaningful intervention capabilities ensure reviewers can address identified issues.

The combination of technical solutions and human oversight creates more robust protection against bias. This dual approach helps organizations identify potential issues early and respond to concerns promptly. Consistent attention to system fairness supports ongoing improvement, while regular adjustment of approaches helps address emerging challenges.

Moving beyond bias detection and mitigation,

organizations must focus on building AI systems that promote fairness from the ground up. This proactive approach embeds fairness considerations into every stage of system development and deployment.

Fair AI systems begin with clear design principles that prioritize equity and inclusion. These principles should guide every decision in the development process, from initial concept through final implementation. Organizations need to establish clear fairness metrics that define success in concrete terms. Inclusive development practices must become standard procedure, while transparent decision processes enable proper oversight.

The established principles must consider both technical and social aspects of fairness. Systems should demonstrate their ability to serve diverse populations effectively, maintaining consistent performance across different groups. Decisions need clear explanations that help users understand outcomes, while meaningful oversight ensures continued alignment with fairness goals.

These foundational principles shape how organizations approach AI development. Regular assessment of principle application helps maintain focus on fairness throughout the development process. Consistent evaluation of outcomes against established principles enables continuous improvement, while regular principle review ensures continued relevance.

Turning principles into practice requires structured approaches to system development. Organizations should establish comprehensive development protocols that ensure diverse team participation throughout the process. Regular bias assessment must become standard practice, while thorough testing confirms system performance across different scenarios.

Testing requirements need careful definition to verify system effectiveness. Performance evaluation across different groups helps ensure consistent fairness in outcomes. Decision consistency requires regular verification, while reliability testing confirms stable performance across various conditions. Impact assessment helps understand broader effects of system deployment.

Monitoring systems play a vital role in maintaining fairness over time. Organizations must track ongoing performance to identify any emerging issues quickly. User feedback provides crucial insight into real-world system impact, while social impact assessment helps understand broader consequences of system deployment.

Successful implementation requires commitment throughout the organization. Leadership must provide necessary resources to support thorough development and testing processes. Support for comprehensive testing ensures proper system evaluation, while meaningful oversight capabilities enable effective response to identified issues. Prompt attention to concerns helps maintain system fairness over time.

Building fair systems represents an ongoing process rather than a one-time achievement. Organizations must maintain vigilance in monitoring system performance and impact. Regular evaluation of implementation practices helps identify areas for improvement, while consistent attention to emerging challenges enables appropriate response to new situations.

As artificial intelligence continues to evolve and influence more aspects of our lives, the challenge of addressing bias takes on increasing importance. Understanding current approaches while preparing for future developments helps organizations maintain fair and effective AI systems.

The landscape of AI bias continues to evolve as technology advances. New applications bring fresh challenges for ensuring fairness. More sophisticated AI systems might introduce subtle forms of bias that prove harder to detect with current methods. The increasing autonomy of AI systems raises new questions about fairness in more complex decision-making processes.

The integration of AI across critical social systems demands particular attention. As these systems take on more significant roles in healthcare, education, and public services, ensuring fairness becomes increasingly crucial. The growing sophistication of AI capabilities requires evolution in our understanding of bias and our approaches to maintaining fairness.

Standards and expectations for fairness continue to develop alongside technological advancement. What constitutes acceptable performance may change as our understanding of bias deepens. Society's expectations for AI fairness may evolve, requiring organizations to adapt their approaches accordingly.

Addressing AI bias requires ongoing commitment to improvement. Organizations must stay informed about emerging challenges in bias detection and mitigation. Understanding of fairness continues to evolve, requiring regular updates to testing and monitoring approaches. Enhancement of mitigation strategies helps address new forms of bias as they emerge.

The field continues to develop new tools and methods for ensuring AI fairness. Advances in bias detection enable more thorough system evaluation. Improved development approaches help create fairer systems from the start. Enhanced monitoring capabilities support better ongoing assessment of system performance and impact.

As we move forward to explore other aspects of AI development in subsequent chapters, the principles of fairness and bias mitigation remain crucial considerations. Understanding how to build and maintain fair AI systems provides essential foundation for responsible AI development and deployment. The challenge of AI bias reflects broader questions about fairness and equity in our society. As we develop more sophisticated AI systems, we must ensure they contribute to creating more equitable outcomes rather than reinforcing existing disparities.

CHAPTER 11: PRIVACY IN THE AGE OF AI

The remarkable capabilities of artificial intelligence we've explored in previous chapters come with a significant cost: an unprecedented appetite for data. As AI systems become more integrated into our daily lives, they collect and process more personal information than ever before, raising crucial questions about privacy in the modern age.

Artificial intelligence thrives on data. The more information AI systems can access and analyze, the better they become at their designated tasks. This fundamental characteristic creates an inherent tension between AI capability and personal privacy. Every interaction with an AI system, from asking a virtual assistant for weather updates to using a navigation app for directions, generates data about our behaviors, preferences, and patterns.

This constant data collection often occurs invisibly in the background of our digital lives. When we scroll through social media, shop online, or use smart home devices, AI systems gather information about our choices and habits. While this data collection enables personalized services and improved functionality, it also raises profound questions about privacy and personal autonomy in an AI-driven world.

The scale of this data gathering extends far beyond what most people realize. Individual pieces of information that might seem innocuous on their own combine to create detailed profiles of our lives. Our shopping habits, location history, search queries, and social interactions all contribute to an increasingly comprehensive digital picture of who we are.

Modern data collection differs fundamentally from traditional information gathering. AI systems don't just collect specific pieces of information for particular purposes. They constantly gather, analyze, and process data, finding patterns and making predictions that might not be apparent even to the individuals providing the information.

Consider how a simple smartphone contains sensors tracking location, movement, and activity patterns. It records our communications, monitors our app usage, and observes our daily routines. Each interaction adds another layer to the detailed profile being built about our lives, preferences, and behaviors.

This comprehensive data collection enables AI systems to provide increasingly sophisticated services. Navigation apps can predict traffic patterns and suggest faster routes. Entertainment services can recommend content tailored to our interests. Healthcare applications can monitor wellness and suggest behavioral changes. Yet each of these conveniences comes with privacy implications that deserve careful consideration.

The privacy challenges we face today differ significantly from those of the past. Traditional privacy concerns focused on keeping specific pieces of information secret. Modern privacy challenges involve managing the constant flow of data generated by our digital lives and understanding how this information might be used, analyzed, and interpreted by AI systems.

As we explore these privacy challenges and their

implications, we must consider both the benefits that AI-driven services provide and the privacy risks they present. Understanding this balance proves crucial for making informed decisions about our interaction with AI systems and our approach to personal privacy in the digital age.

The methods AI systems use to collect data have become increasingly sophisticated and pervasive. Understanding these collection methods helps us grasp both the capabilities of modern AI and its implications for personal privacy.

Every time we venture online, we leave digital footprints that AI systems collect and analyze. Our browsing history creates a map of our interests and concerns. The time we spend on different websites indicates our engagement levels and preferences. Even our cursor movements and scrolling patterns provide information about our behavior and decision-making processes.

Search engines track not just what we search for, but how we phrase our queries and which results we select. This information helps AI systems understand not just our immediate interests, but our thought processes and decision-making patterns. The advertisements we click, the products we view, and the articles we read all contribute to an increasingly detailed profile of our preferences and behaviors.

Our smart devices have become sophisticated data collection tools. Smartphones track our location, movement patterns, and daily routines. They monitor our communication patterns, app usage, and even how we hold and interact with the device itself. This constant stream of data provides AI systems with intimate details about our daily lives and habits.

Smart home devices extend this data collection into our living spaces. Voice-activated assistants listen for commands but also gather data about our home activities and routines. Smart thermostats learn our temperature preferences and daily patterns. Security cameras with AI capabilities monitor movement and activity patterns. Each device adds another layer to the detailed picture of our private lives.

Wearable technology brings data collection even closer to our physical selves. Fitness trackers monitor our exercise habits, sleep patterns, and vital signs. Smart watches track our movement and activity levels throughout the day. These devices provide AI systems with intimate details about our physical health and daily routines.

Social media platforms represent perhaps the most comprehensive source of personal data collection. These platforms don't just record our explicit actions like posts and likes; they analyze our browsing patterns, the time we spend viewing different types of content, and our interactions with other users.

The integration of AI into social media platforms enables increasingly sophisticated analysis of our behavior. Systems track not just what content we engage with, but how long we pause on different items, what causes us to stop scrolling, and what prompts us to interact. This detailed behavioral data helps AI systems build increasingly accurate models of our preferences and tendencies.

Even our social connections become data points for analysis. AI systems examine our interaction patterns with friends and followers, the timing and nature of our communications, and the spread of content through our social networks. This social graph provides valuable insight into our relationships, influences, and community connections.

The combination of these various data collection methods creates an unprecedented level of insight into individual lives. While each method might seem limited in scope, the aggregate effect produces detailed profiles that can reveal surprising aspects of our personalities, preferences, and behaviors. Understanding this comprehensive nature of modern data collection proves crucial for making informed decisions about privacy in the AI era.

Once AI systems collect data, they process and use this information in ways that extend far beyond simple storage and retrieval. Understanding how AI systems use our data reveals both the benefits and privacy implications of modern data processing.

AI systems collect data with specific purposes in mind, though these purposes often expand over time. The primary goal typically involves improving system performance and user experience. When a streaming service tracks viewing habits, it aims to provide better content recommendations. When a navigation app monitors travel patterns, it works to suggest more efficient routes.

However, the sophistication of AI analysis means that collected data often reveals more than its original purpose might suggest. Shopping data might indicate significant life changes like marriage or pregnancy before a person announces such news. Location data might reveal social connections, daily routines, or even health conditions through patterns of movement and activity.

The predictive capabilities of AI systems transform seemingly basic data into powerful tools for understanding and anticipating human behavior. Systems analyze patterns to predict future actions, preferences, and needs. This predictive power offers convenience but raises questions about personal autonomy and privacy.

Data rarely remains confined to its original collection point. Modern AI systems often share and combine information across platforms and applications. Your search history might influence the advertisements you see on social media. Your purchase history might affect the content recommendations you receive on streaming services.

The flow of information through AI systems creates complex networks of data sharing and analysis. Organizations process collected data through various AI models and algorithms, each extracting different insights and patterns. These insights then inform various applications and services, often in ways not immediately apparent to users.

This sophisticated data processing enables increasingly personalized services but also raises privacy concerns. The combination of data from multiple sources can reveal sensitive information even when individual data points seem harmless. A person's interests, habits, and even personal circumstances might become apparent through pattern analysis across different data sources.

The speed and scale of modern data processing add another dimension to privacy considerations. AI systems can analyze vast amounts of data in real-time, making immediate decisions based on current and historical information. This capability enables responsive services but also means that privacy implications occur instantly and continuously.

Understanding these data uses and flows proves crucial for managing personal privacy in the AI era. While individual pieces of shared information might seem insignificant, their combination and analysis through AI systems can create detailed insights into personal lives. This reality requires careful consideration of how we share and allow the use of our personal information.

The extensive data collection and processing capabilities of AI systems create significant privacy risks. These concerns extend beyond traditional data security to fundamental questions about personal privacy in an AI-driven world.

The concentration of personal data in AI systems creates attractive targets for malicious actors. Data breaches can expose sensitive personal information, from financial details to health records. The comprehensive nature of modern data collection means that a single breach might reveal intimate details about many aspects of a person's life.

Traditional security measures often prove insufficient for protecting AI-processed data. The complexity of modern AI systems creates multiple potential vulnerability points. Even when core systems remain secure, data might be exposed through third-party applications, data transfer processes, or human error. The interconnected nature of AI systems means that a breach in one area can compromise data across multiple domains.

146

AI BASICS: THE FUNDAMENTALS

The potential impact of security breaches grows more severe as AI systems collect more comprehensive personal information. When systems combine data from multiple sources, security failures can expose not just individual data points but detailed profiles of personal lives. A breach might reveal not only what people do but predict what they might do, based on AI analysis of their patterns and behaviors.

Beyond security concerns lie deeper questions about data control and ownership. Once personal information enters AI systems, individuals often lose practical control over how their data gets used and shared. The sophistication of AI analysis means that even seemingly anonymous data might reveal personal information when combined with other sources.

Third-party sharing of data raises particular concerns. AI systems often share information with partner organizations, advertisers, or other services. Each sharing instance creates new privacy risks and reduces individual control over personal information. The complexity of modern data sharing networks makes it difficult for individuals to track or manage how their information spreads.

The permanence of digital data adds another layer of concern. Information collected by AI systems might persist indefinitely, analyzed and reanalyzed as technology advances. Today's seemingly innocent data might reveal unexpected insights through future AI capabilities. This potential for future analysis creates privacy risks that extend well beyond current concerns.

Surveillance capabilities enabled by AI technology raise additional privacy issues. Facial recognition systems, behavior analysis algorithms, and location tracking create unprecedented abilities to monitor individual activities. The combination of these technologies with extensive data collection enables detailed tracking of personal movements, activities, and associations.

These privacy risks carry real-world consequences. Exposed personal information might affect employment opportunities, insurance availability, or social relationships. AI analysis of collected data might influence credit decisions, healthcare access, or educational opportunities. The impact extends beyond immediate privacy concerns to long-term personal and professional implications.

Understanding privacy risks leads naturally to the question of protection. While complete privacy proves increasingly difficult in our AI-driven world, various strategies can help individuals maintain reasonable control over their personal information.

Personal privacy protection begins with mindful data sharing. Every interaction with AI systems presents choices about what information to share. Simple actions like adjusting privacy settings on devices and applications can significantly reduce unnecessary data collection. Taking time to understand and configure these settings helps establish basic privacy boundaries.

Managing permissions requires regular attention. Applications frequently request access to various types of personal data, from location information to contact lists. Critically evaluating these requests and granting access only when necessary helps limit data exposure. Regular review and updates of permission settings ensure continued privacy protection as applications evolve.

Strong authentication practices provide another crucial layer of protection. Using unique, complex passwords for different services reduces vulnerability to security breaches. Two-factor authentication adds significant protection by requiring additional verification beyond passwords. These basic security measures help prevent unauthorized access to personal information.

Understanding privacy policies and terms of service, though often tedious, proves increasingly important. These documents reveal how organizations collect, use, and share personal data. While few people read these policies in detail, even basic familiarity helps inform decisions about which services to use and what information to share.

Technical protection measures complement personal privacy practices. Privacy-focused browsers and search engines limit tracking of online activities. Ad blockers and tracking prevention tools reduce data collection during web browsing. Encryption tools protect sensitive communications and stored information.

Virtual Private Networks (VPNs) provide additional privacy protection by masking internet activity from surveillance. Privacy-focused email services offer alternatives to platforms that scan message content for advertising purposes. Secure messaging applications enable private communication with strong encryption.

Regular device maintenance supports privacy protection. Updating software ensures security patches remain current. Removing unused applications reduces potential data collection points. Regular review and clearing of accumulated data prevents unnecessary information storage.

These technical measures require balance between protection and convenience. While maximum privacy might suggest avoiding AI-driven services entirely, practical modern life often requires their use. The goal becomes finding appropriate balance between utilizing beneficial services while maintaining reasonable privacy protection.

Effective privacy protection combines both personal practices and technical measures. Understanding available tools and protection strategies enables informed decisions about data sharing. Regular attention to privacy measures helps maintain protection as technology evolves and new challenges emerge.

As AI systems collect and process more personal information, governments worldwide have begun establishing regulatory frameworks to protect individual privacy. These regulations shape how organizations collect, use, and protect personal data.

The European Union's General Data Protection

Regulation (GDPR) represents one of the most comprehensive approaches to data privacy protection. This regulation establishes fundamental rights regarding personal data, including the right to know what information organizations collect and how they use it. It requires explicit consent for data collection and provides individuals with rights to access, correct, and delete their personal information.

Other regions have developed their own privacy regulations. California's Consumer Privacy Act provides similar protections for state residents. China's Personal Information Protection Law establishes strict requirements for data handling. These varying regulations create a complex landscape for organizations operating across international boundaries.

Current regulations typically address several key areas. They establish requirements for data collection consent, ensuring organizations clearly explain their data practices. They define responsibilities for data protection, requiring appropriate security measures. They specify individual rights regarding personal information, enabling greater control over collected data.

Privacy regulation continues to evolve as technology advances. New AI capabilities create novel privacy challenges requiring regulatory attention. The increasing sophistication of data analysis and prediction capabilities raises questions about what constitutes personal information requiring protection.

Emerging regulations focus increasingly on AI-specific privacy concerns. These include restrictions on automated decision-making, requirements for algorithmic transparency, and protections against surveillance technologies. Future regulations will likely address emerging technologies like advanced facial recognition, behavior prediction, and emotional analysis.

The global nature of AI technology creates pressure for international privacy standards. While different regions maintain distinct approaches, organizations increasingly need consistent privacy practices across jurisdictions. This drives development of common principles and practices for privacy protection.

Regulatory developments affect both organizations and individuals. Companies must adapt their practices to meet evolving requirements, often implementing more robust privacy protections. Individuals gain new rights and protections, though exercising these rights requires understanding and engagement with privacy regulations.

The interaction between regulation and innovation requires careful balance. While privacy protection remains crucial, overly restrictive regulations might limit beneficial AI development. Future regulatory frameworks must protect privacy while enabling continued technological advancement.

Privacy protection in the age of AI represents an ongoing challenge that will continue to evolve as technology advances. Understanding current privacy concerns while anticipating future developments helps prepare for coming changes in the AI privacy landscape.

AI capabilities continue to expand, creating new privacy challenges. Advanced natural language processing may enable more sophisticated analysis of personal communications. Improved pattern recognition could reveal more detailed insights from seemingly basic data. Emotional analysis and behavior prediction raise novel questions about personal privacy boundaries.

The integration of AI into more aspects of daily life will likely increase privacy concerns. Smart cities might collect detailed information about citizen movements and activities. Advanced healthcare monitoring could gather intimate details about personal health and behavior. Workplace AI might track employee performance and interaction patterns in unprecedented detail.

These advancing capabilities suggest privacy protection will require continuing attention and adaptation. Current protection strategies may need revision as AI systems develop new ways to collect and analyze personal information. Individual privacy practices will need regular updates to address emerging challenges.

The future of AI privacy requires careful balance between competing interests. The benefits of AI-driven services often depend on access to personal information. Medical diagnosis improvements need detailed health data. Traffic optimization requires location information. Entertainment personalization relies on preference data.

This balance extends beyond individual services to broader societal benefits. AI advances in scientific research, public safety, and environmental protection may require extensive data collection. Understanding these tradeoffs helps inform decisions about acceptable privacy compromises.

Education about privacy implications becomes increasingly important as AI technology evolves. People need understanding of both risks and protection strategies to make informed decisions about personal information sharing. This knowledge helps individuals maintain appropriate privacy while benefiting from AI advances.

As we move forward, privacy considerations will remain crucial in AI development and deployment. The challenges explored in this chapter provide foundation for understanding both current privacy issues and future concerns. This knowledge proves essential for navigating personal privacy in an increasingly AI-enhanced world.

CHAPTER 12: RESPONSIBLE AI

As artificial intelligence systems take on increasingly significant roles in society, the need for responsible development and deployment becomes crucial. The power to influence decisions affecting people's lives brings with it an obligation to ensure AI systems operate ethically and responsibly.

The impact of AI extends far beyond technical performance into questions of ethics, fairness, and social responsibility. When AI systems make decisions about loans, jobs, medical treatment, or legal matters, they affect real lives in profound ways. Every AI deployment carries potential for both benefit and harm, making responsible development essential rather than optional.

As we've seen in previous chapters, AI systems can inadvertently perpetuate biases, compromise privacy, or make decisions that significantly impact individuals and communities. The increasing autonomy and capability of these systems raises stakes for ensuring their responsible development and use. Understanding what constitutes responsible AI helps organizations create systems that benefit society while minimizing potential harm.

The scope of AI influence makes responsible development a societal imperative rather than just a technical challenge. As these systems integrate more deeply into crucial social systems like healthcare, education, and public services, their potential impact on human lives and communities grows. This reality demands careful consideration of how AI systems are designed, deployed, and monitored.

Responsible AI encompasses more than just technical excellence or operational efficiency. It requires developing and deploying AI systems in ways that respect human rights, ensure fairness, maintain transparency, and promote positive societal impact. This approach considers not just what AI can do, but what it should do and how it should operate.

At its core, responsible AI focuses on ensuring that artificial intelligence serves human values and societal benefit. This means creating systems that not only perform their intended functions effectively but do so in ways that respect individual rights, promote fairness, and maintain accountability. These considerations must be built into AI systems from their initial design through ongoing operation.

The concept extends beyond individual organizations to industry-wide standards and practices. While specific implementations might vary, certain fundamental principles emerge as essential for responsible AI development. These include ensuring fairness in system outcomes, maintaining transparency in decision-making processes, establishing clear accountability for system actions, protecting privacy, and prioritizing safety.

The development and deployment of responsible AI systems rests on several fundamental principles. These principles provide a framework for ensuring AI systems benefit society while minimizing potential harm.

Fairness in AI systems extends beyond simple equal treatment. It requires careful attention to how systems affect different groups and individuals. As we explored in our discussion of AI bias, achieving fairness means ensuring AI systems don't disadvantage particular groups or perpetuate existing social inequities.

Creating fair AI systems requires consideration throughout the development process. This begins with representative data collection and continues through system design, testing, and deployment. Organizations must regularly assess their systems' impact across different populations, ensuring consistent and equitable treatment for all users.

The pursuit of fairness often reveals complex tradeoffs. Different definitions of fairness might conflict with each other, requiring careful consideration of how to balance competing objectives. What appears fair from one perspective might create unintended consequences from another, demanding thoughtful analysis and decision-making.

Transparency enables understanding of how AI systems make decisions. When systems affect important aspects of people's lives, those affected deserve to understand how decisions are made. This understanding proves particularly crucial in areas like healthcare, finance, and legal applications.

Achieving meaningful transparency requires more than just technical openness. Systems must explain their decisions in ways that relevant stakeholders can understand. This might mean different levels of explanation for different audiences, technical details for system auditors, clear explanations for affected individuals, and appropriate oversight information for regulators.

The challenge of transparency grows with system complexity. Advanced AI systems might make decisions based on intricate patterns that prove difficult to explain in simple terms. Finding ways to make these decisions understandable while maintaining system sophistication represents an ongoing challenge in responsible AI development.

Clear accountability ensures responsibility for AI system decisions and actions. Organizations deploying AI systems must maintain clear lines of responsibility for system outcomes. This includes establishing who holds accountability for system decisions and how to address issues when they arise.

Accountability extends throughout the AI development and deployment process. Organizations need clear protocols for addressing problems, correcting errors, and managing consequences of system decisions. This includes mechanisms for affected individuals to challenge decisions and seek redress when necessary.

Effective accountability requires ongoing monitoring and evaluation of AI systems. Organizations must track system performance, assess outcomes, and maintain clear documentation of decision processes. This enables proper oversight and ensures ability to address issues as they emerge.

Privacy protection builds on our previous discussion of AI privacy concerns. Responsible AI development requires careful attention to data collection, usage, and protection. Systems must respect individual privacy rights while maintaining necessary functionality.

Organizations need clear policies governing data handling throughout the AI lifecycle. This includes specifications for data collection, storage, processing, and deletion. Privacy protection must consider not just direct data usage but also potential inference and combination of data from multiple sources.

Safety in AI systems encompasses both physical and social aspects. Systems must operate within clear safety boundaries, whether controlling physical equipment or making decisions affecting human welfare. This requires robust testing, careful monitoring, and clear protocols for addressing safety concerns.

Safety considerations extend beyond immediate system operation to longer-term impacts. Organizations must consider potential consequences of system deployment, including unintended effects on individuals and communities.

This forward-looking approach helps prevent harmful outcomes before they occur.

Moving from principles to practice requires concrete approaches for implementing responsible AI. Organizations must translate ethical guidelines into specific development and deployment practices that ensure responsible operation of AI systems.

Many organizations establish dedicated ethics boards to oversee AI development and deployment. These boards typically include diverse perspectives, bringing together technical experts, ethicists, legal specialists, and domain experts. This diversity helps ensure comprehensive consideration of potential impacts and implications of AI systems.

Ethics review processes need integration throughout the AI development lifecycle. Rather than treating ethical review as a final checkpoint, organizations should incorporate ethical consideration from initial concept through deployment and ongoing operation. This integrated approach helps identify and address potential issues early in development.

Internal guidelines play a crucial role in implementing responsible AI practices. Organizations need clear standards for development teams, including specific criteria for assessing fairness, transparency, and accountability. These guidelines should provide practical direction while maintaining flexibility for different applications and contexts.

Responsible AI development requires specific technical practices to ensure ethical principles translate into system operation. Development teams need concrete methods for testing fairness, implementing transparency, and maintaining accountability in their systems.

Testing protocols must verify system performance across different populations and scenarios. This includes comprehensive evaluation of system behavior under various conditions and with diverse user groups. Regular testing throughout development helps identify potential issues before they affect real-world operations.

Quality assurance for responsible AI extends beyond traditional software testing. Teams must verify not just technical functionality but also ethical compliance. This might include specific tests for bias, assessments of decision transparency, and evaluation of privacy protection measures.

Documentation proves essential for maintaining responsible AI practices. Development teams must maintain clear records of design decisions, testing procedures, and system behaviors. This documentation supports both internal oversight and external accountability, enabling proper evaluation of system operation and impact.

The verification of ethical compliance requires specific technical tools and methods. Organizations need ways to monitor system behavior, assess fairness metrics, and evaluate transparency measures. These technical capabilities support ongoing assessment of responsible operation.

Implementation challenges often emerge when translating ethical principles into technical solutions. Teams must balance competing requirements while maintaining system effectiveness. This might involve tradeoffs between model accuracy and explainability, or between personalization and privacy protection.

Regular assessment and adjustment of implementation practices helps maintain responsible operation as systems evolve. Organizations must monitor system performance, evaluate impacts, and update practices based on observed outcomes. This ongoing process ensures continued alignment with responsible AI principles.

As AI systems become more prevalent and influential, regulatory frameworks emerge to govern their development and deployment. These frameworks help ensure responsible AI practices while providing guidance for organizations implementing AI systems.

The European Union leads many regulatory efforts with comprehensive approaches to AI governance. The EU's AI

Act represents one of the first major attempts to create a unified framework for regulating artificial intelligence. This regulation categorizes AI applications based on risk levels, applying stricter requirements to systems with greater potential for harm.

Different regions approach AI regulation in varying ways. Some focus on specific applications, like facial recognition or automated decision-making systems. Others establish broader frameworks addressing AI development and deployment generally. These varying approaches create a complex landscape for organizations operating across multiple jurisdictions.

Industry standards complement government regulations in promoting responsible AI practices. Professional organizations and industry groups develop guidelines for ethical AI development. These standards often provide more specific technical guidance than government regulations, helping organizations implement responsible practices.

Current regulatory frameworks typically address several key areas. Privacy protection builds on existing data protection laws like GDPR. Fairness requirements ensure non-discrimination in AI decision-making. Transparency guidelines mandate explanations for significant automated decisions. Safety standards establish requirements for AI systems in critical applications.

Regulatory approaches continue to evolve as our understanding of AI capabilities and impact continues to grow. New standards emerge to address previously unrecognized challenges. Existing frameworks adapt to accommodate technological advances and changing societal needs.

Future regulations will likely focus increasingly on specific AI capabilities and applications. Autonomous system operation, emotional analysis, and behavior prediction raise novel regulatory concerns. Standards for these emerging capabilities must balance innovation with protection of individual rights and societal interests.

International coordination in AI regulation gains importance as systems operate across borders. While different regions maintain distinct approaches, pressure grows for harmonized standards. Organizations increasingly need consistent frameworks for responsible AI development and deployment.

The development of technical standards supports regulatory compliance. These standards provide specific methods for implementing regulatory requirements. They help organizations translate high-level principles into practical development and deployment practices.

Regular updates to regulatory frameworks prove essential as AI technology advances. New capabilities create novel challenges requiring regulatory attention. Existing standards need revision to address emerging issues and changing technological contexts.

While the principles and frameworks for responsible AI provide clear direction, organizations face significant challenges in practical implementation. Understanding these challenges helps develop more effective approaches to responsible AI development and deployment.

The complexity of modern AI systems creates fundamental challenges for responsible implementation. As systems become more sophisticated, understanding and explaining their decision-making processes grows more difficult. This complexity affects ability to ensure transparency and maintain appropriate oversight of system operation.

System monitoring presents particular challenges. Organizations must track not just technical performance but also ethical compliance across numerous dimensions. Detecting potential bias, verifying fair operation, and ensuring privacy protection require sophisticated monitoring capabilities. These requirements often stretch beyond traditional technical metrics and testing approaches.

The dynamic nature of AI systems adds another layer of

complexity. Systems that learn and adapt over time may develop unexpected behaviors or biases. Maintaining responsible operation requires continuous monitoring and adjustment rather than one-time verification. Organizations must develop methods for ongoing assessment and correction of system behavior.

Resource requirements for responsible AI implementation often exceed initial expectations. Organizations need specialized expertise in both technical development and ethical assessment. Building and maintaining appropriate oversight systems requires significant investment. These resource demands can challenge organizations' ability to maintain comprehensive responsible AI practices.

Balancing competing priorities creates ongoing challenges. Organizations must weigh system performance against ethical requirements, often facing difficult tradeoffs. Transparency might conflict with system sophistication. Privacy protection might limit functionality. Finding appropriate balance points requires careful consideration and sometimes difficult choices.

The pace of technological change creates additional implementation challenges. New capabilities emerge before clear guidelines for their responsible use develop. Organizations must often make decisions about responsible implementation without established frameworks or best practices. This requires careful judgment and willingness to adjust approaches as understanding evolves.

Cultural and organizational changes often prove necessary for effective implementation of responsible AI practices. Development teams need new skills and perspectives. Decision-making processes must incorporate ethical considerations. Organizations must build cultures that value responsible development alongside technical achievement.

Integration with existing systems and processes presents practical challenges. Organizations must adapt current development practices to incorporate responsible AI requirements. This adaptation affects everything from project planning to quality assurance. Successfully managing these changes while maintaining operational effectiveness requires careful planning and execution.

The development of responsible AI practices continues to evolve as technology advances and our understanding deepens. Looking ahead helps organizations prepare for emerging challenges while strengthening current approaches to responsible AI implementation.

Responsible AI standards will likely become more sophisticated as experience with AI implementation grows. Current frameworks provide foundation for more detailed and nuanced approaches. Organizations and regulators learn from practical experience, developing more effective guidelines for responsible development and deployment.

Technical capabilities for implementing responsible AI continue to advance. New tools emerge for monitoring system behavior and assessing ethical compliance. Improved methods for explaining AI decisions help address transparency challenges. These advancing capabilities enable more effective implementation of responsible AI principles.

The scope of responsible AI considerations expands as AI capabilities grow. Emerging technologies like advanced natural language processing and autonomous systems create novel ethical challenges. Standards and practices must evolve to address these new capabilities while maintaining fundamental principles of responsible development.

Organizations must prepare for increasing emphasis on responsible AI practices. This preparation involves building stronger internal capabilities for ethical assessment and implementation. Teams need enhanced skills in both technical development and ethical consideration. Leadership must strengthen commitment to responsible practices while maintaining innovation and effectiveness.

Industry collaboration becomes increasingly important for advancing responsible AI practices. Organizations can learn from shared experiences and challenges. Common approaches to implementing responsible AI help establish consistent standards across the field. This collaboration supports more effective development of responsible AI systems.

Education and training take on greater importance as responsible AI practices mature. Technical teams need deeper understanding of ethical implications in their work. Leadership requires better appreciation of responsible AI challenges and requirements. Organizations must invest in developing these capabilities throughout their structure.

The future of responsible AI depends on maintaining balance between innovation and ethical consideration. Organizations must find ways to advance AI capabilities while ensuring responsible development and deployment. This balance requires ongoing attention to both technological possibilities and ethical implications.

Looking ahead, responsible AI practices will likely become more integrated into standard development processes. Rather than treating ethical considerations as additional requirements, organizations will incorporate them naturally into their approach to AI development and deployment. This integration helps ensure more effective implementation of responsible AI principles.

CHAPTER 13: AI FOR GOOD

While previous chapters have explored artificial intelligence's technical capabilities and operational considerations, we now turn to examine how these technologies can address some of humanity's most pressing challenges. The application of AI for social benefit represents one of the most promising aspects of this technological revolution.

AI for Good represents more than just technological application—it embodies the deliberate use of artificial intelligence to address global challenges and improve human welfare. This approach focuses on leveraging AI capabilities not merely for commercial or operational efficiency, but for tackling fundamental issues facing humanity: climate change, healthcare access, poverty, hunger, and disaster response.

The concept extends beyond individual applications to encompass collaborative efforts between governments, research institutions, non-profit organizations, and private enterprises. These partnerships bring together diverse expertise and resources, enabling more comprehensive approaches to complex global challenges. The combination of technological capability with humanitarian focus creates opportunities for meaningful impact on a global scale.

The scope of AI for Good initiatives ranges from local interventions to global programs. Some projects address specific community needs, like improving crop yields for small farmers. Others tackle broader challenges, such as developing early warning systems for natural disasters or creating more accessible healthcare solutions for underserved populations.

The potential impact of AI for Good initiatives proves particularly significant because these technologies can scale efficiently once developed. A successful solution in one region can often be adapted and deployed in others, multiplying its beneficial impact. This scalability makes AI particularly valuable for addressing widespread challenges that affect multiple communities or regions.

Current applications demonstrate the breadth of possible impact. AI systems analyze satellite data to predict environmental changes, process medical images to detect diseases earlier, optimize resource distribution for humanitarian aid, and improve agricultural practices for better food security. Each application represents not just technological achievement but meaningful improvement in people's lives.

The collaborative nature of AI for Good initiatives often leads to innovative approaches that might not emerge from purely commercial development. When organizations focus on social impact rather than just profit, they often discover novel applications and creative solutions. This alternative perspective helps drive both technological advancement and social benefit.

As we explore specific applications in subsequent sections, we'll see how AI capabilities align with humanitarian needs. Understanding this alignment helps reveal both current achievements and future possibilities for applying artificial intelligence to global challenges.

AI BASICS: THE FUNDAMENTALS

Among global challenges, climate change stands as one of the most pressing issues facing humanity. Artificial intelligence provides powerful tools for both understanding climate change and developing responses to its effects.

Modern climate science requires processing vast amounts of environmental data from diverse sources. AI systems analyze information from satellites, weather stations, ocean buoys, and ground sensors to identify patterns and predict environmental changes. This capability enables more accurate understanding of climate trends and their potential impacts.

NASA and other space agencies employ AI systems to process satellite imagery for tracking environmental changes. These systems monitor everything from Arctic ice coverage to deforestation patterns in real time. The ability to process and analyze this data quickly helps scientists understand climate change progression and identify areas requiring immediate attention.

Weather prediction has evolved significantly through AI application. Advanced modeling systems now predict extreme weather events with greater accuracy and longer lead times. These predictions prove crucial for communities preparing for hurricanes, floods, or droughts. The improved accuracy and earlier warnings help save lives and protect resources in vulnerable areas.

AI technologies play an increasingly important role in addressing one of the primary contributors to climate change: energy usage. Smart grid systems employing AI optimize power distribution, reducing waste and improving efficiency across power networks. These systems balance power supply and demand in real time, enabling better integration of renewable energy sources.

Major technology companies demonstrate the potential for AI in energy optimization. Google's implementation of AI systems for data center cooling achieved significant energy reductions while maintaining performance. This application shows how AI can help large facilities reduce their environmental impact while maintaining operational effectiveness.

Renewable energy integration benefits particularly from AI capabilities. These systems help manage the variable nature of solar and wind power, predicting generation capacity and optimizing storage systems. AI-driven forecasting helps power companies balance renewable sources with traditional power generation, enabling greater reliance on clean energy.

Transportation systems represent another area where AI supports climate change mitigation. Smart traffic management systems reduce vehicle emissions by optimizing traffic flow. AI-powered logistics systems plan more efficient delivery routes, reducing fuel consumption and emissions from commercial transportation.

The combination of these applications creates comprehensive approaches to energy management and emissions reduction. From individual buildings to city-wide systems, AI helps optimize energy usage and reduce environmental impact. These applications demonstrate how technological capability can directly address environmental challenges.

The application of artificial intelligence to healthcare represents one of the most promising areas for positive social impact. AI technologies create opportunities for improving both the quality and accessibility of healthcare services worldwide.

Early disease detection often makes the difference between successful treatment and poor outcomes. AI systems have demonstrated remarkable capabilities in analyzing medical images, identifying potential issues before they become apparent to human observers. Systems analyzing mammograms can detect early signs of breast cancer, while others examine chest X-rays for indicators of tuberculosis or lung cancer.

DeepMind's work in medical imaging illustrates the potential of these applications. Their AI models have achieved accuracy rates matching or exceeding human experts in detecting various conditions. These capabilities prove particularly valuable in regions with limited access to specialist physicians, enabling earlier detection and treatment of serious conditions.

Beyond image analysis, AI systems process various types of medical data to identify potential health issues. These systems analyze patient records, test results, and genetic information to identify risk factors and predict potential health problems. This predictive capability enables preventive interventions, potentially stopping diseases before they develop.

Telemedicine supported by AI creates new possibilities for healthcare delivery, particularly in underserved areas. During the COVID-19 pandemic, AI-powered screening systems helped healthcare providers manage the surge in patient inquiries while maintaining quality care. These systems demonstrate how technology can extend healthcare services beyond traditional facilities.

Remote diagnosis capabilities prove particularly valuable in regions lacking specialist physicians. AI systems can analyze patient symptoms and medical data, providing initial assessments and recommendations for care. While these systems don't replace human medical professionals, they help prioritize cases and ensure more efficient use of limited medical resources.

AI systems also improve healthcare efficiency through better resource management. From predicting patient admission rates to optimizing medical supply distribution, these applications help healthcare facilities operate more effectively. This efficiency proves particularly crucial in regions with limited healthcare resources.

The combination of improved detection capabilities and enhanced healthcare access creates opportunities for better health outcomes globally. AI technologies help address disparities in healthcare availability while improving the quality of care available to all populations. These applications demonstrate technology's potential to address fundamental human needs.

The application of artificial intelligence to disaster response demonstrates how technology can help save lives and protect communities during critical situations. From predicting natural disasters to coordinating relief efforts, AI systems provide valuable tools for emergency management.

Early warning systems powered by AI analyze multiple data sources to predict potential disasters. The United States Geological Survey employs AI systems to process seismic data, identifying patterns that might indicate impending earthquakes. Similar systems monitor weather patterns for signs of developing hurricanes or conditions likely to spawn tornadoes.

Wildfire prevention benefits from AI analysis of satellite imagery and environmental data. These systems identify high-risk conditions and potential fire starts, enabling faster response to developing situations. By combining weather data, vegetation conditions, and historical fire patterns, AI helps fire management teams allocate resources more effectively.

Flood prediction systems demonstrate particularly powerful applications of AI technology. By analyzing rainfall patterns, river levels, and topographical data, these systems provide earlier and more accurate flood warnings. This advanced notice gives communities crucial time to prepare and evacuate when necessary.

When disasters strike, AI systems help coordinate complex relief operations. The United Nations and major humanitarian organizations use AI-powered systems to assess damage, identify areas of greatest need, and optimize resource distribution. These capabilities prove particularly valuable in the crucial early hours of disaster response.

Drone technology combined with AI analysis provides rapid assessment of disaster impacts. AI systems process aerial imagery to identify damaged infrastructure, blocked roads, and areas requiring immediate assistance. This quick assessment helps response teams plan effective relief operations and reach affected populations more quickly.

Resource management during disasters benefits significantly from AI assistance. Systems tracking supply availability, transportation routes, and changing needs help ensure efficient distribution of critical supplies. This optimization proves especially important when normal infrastructure suffers damage or disruption.

The World Food Programme exemplifies effective use of AI in humanitarian response. Their systems analyze various data sources to predict where food shortages might occur and plan appropriate responses. This proactive approach helps prevent humanitarian crises from escalating while ensuring more effective use of limited resources.

The application of artificial intelligence to issues of poverty and hunger demonstrates how technology can address fundamental human needs. These applications help improve food production, optimize resource distribution, and support economic development in vulnerable communities.

Modern agriculture benefits significantly from AI-powered optimization. IBM's Watson Decision Platform for Agriculture exemplifies how AI can help farmers improve crop yields while managing resources more efficiently. These systems analyze soil conditions, weather patterns, and crop health to provide specific recommendations for farming practices.

Smart farming applications extend beyond large commercial operations to support small-scale farmers in developing regions. AI systems accessible through mobile devices help farmers identify plant diseases, optimize irrigation, and determine the best times for planting and harvesting. This technology makes advanced agricultural knowledge available to communities that might otherwise lack access to agricultural expertise.

Water management proves particularly crucial for

agricultural success. AI systems help farmers optimize irrigation practices by analyzing soil moisture, weather forecasts, and crop requirements. This precise resource management helps improve yields while conserving crucial water resources, particularly important in regions facing water scarcity.

The challenge of hunger often involves not just food production but efficient distribution of available resources. AI systems help humanitarian organizations optimize their supply chains, ensuring food and other essential resources reach communities in need. The World Food Programme's application of AI for logistics demonstrates how technology can improve the effectiveness of aid distribution.

Market analysis powered by AI helps identify developing food security issues before they become crises. These systems analyze various indicators, from crop prices to weather patterns, predicting potential shortages and enabling proactive responses. This early warning capability helps organizations respond more effectively to developing situations.

Economic development initiatives benefit from AI-powered analysis of poverty patterns and intervention effectiveness. These systems help organizations identify which programs prove most effective in different contexts, enabling more efficient use of limited resources. The ability to analyze complex socioeconomic data helps guide more effective poverty reduction efforts.

Microfinance and economic opportunity programs use AI to extend services to previously underserved populations. Systems analyzing alternative data sources help assess creditworthiness for individuals lacking traditional financial records. This capability helps provide economic opportunities to communities traditionally excluded from financial services.

While current applications of AI for social good already demonstrate significant impact, emerging capabilities suggest even greater potential for addressing global challenges. Understanding these developing applications helps reveal the expanding possibilities for positive social impact through artificial intelligence.

Conservation efforts represent one promising area for expanded AI application. Advanced systems already help track endangered species and monitor ecosystem changes. Future applications might combine multiple data sources with sophisticated analysis to predict environmental threats and guide preservation efforts more effectively. These capabilities could prove crucial for protecting biodiversity and maintaining ecological balance.

Education presents another frontier for AI development. While current systems provide basic personalization of learning experiences, future applications might offer more sophisticated adaptation to individual learning styles and needs. These systems could help address educational inequalities by providing high-quality, personalized learning experiences to students worldwide, regardless of their location or economic circumstances.

Global health monitoring systems demonstrate significant potential for expansion. AI systems might integrate data from various sources to identify emerging health threats before they become crises. The ability to analyze patterns across multiple regions could help prevent disease outbreaks and enable more effective public health responses.

The evolution of AI capabilities suggests new possibilities for addressing social challenges. As systems become more sophisticated in processing and analyzing complex data, they might identify previously unrecognized patterns and solutions. This enhanced understanding could lead to more effective approaches for addressing persistent social issues.

Integration of different AI applications might create more comprehensive solutions. Systems combining climate analysis with agricultural optimization could help communities adapt to changing environmental conditions. Healthcare systems integrated with resource distribution networks might enable more effective delivery of medical services to remote areas.

The democratization of AI technology could expand its positive impact. As tools become more accessible and easier to implement, more communities might develop solutions tailored to their specific needs. This broader participation in AI development could lead to more diverse and effective approaches to social challenges.

Local adaptation of AI solutions represents another promising direction. While global systems provide valuable capabilities, the ability to adjust solutions for specific community contexts proves crucial for effectiveness. Future development might focus on creating systems that more easily adapt to local conditions and needs.

The application of artificial intelligence to global challenges represents one of technology's most promising developments. As we look to the future, understanding both current achievements and future possibilities helps guide continued development of AI for social benefit.

The scope of AI applications for social good continues to grow as technology evolves. What begins as solutions to specific challenges often reveals possibilities for broader application. Climate monitoring systems might inform agricultural development. Healthcare innovations might support disaster response. This cross-pollination of solutions suggests expanding possibilities for positive impact.

Current successes in applying AI to global challenges provide valuable lessons for future development. We learn not just which technical approaches prove effective, but how to implement solutions in ways that respect local contexts and needs. These insights help guide development of more effective and appropriate solutions for diverse communities.

Collaboration between different sectors remains crucial for expanding AI's positive impact. Continued partnership between research institutions, government agencies, private organizations, and local communities helps ensure development of effective and appropriate solutions. These collaborative approaches combine technical capability with practical understanding of community needs.

The future of AI for social benefit depends not just on technological advancement but on maintaining focus on humanitarian needs. As capabilities expand, keeping sight of fundamental human needs and values helps ensure technology serves genuine social benefit. This focus helps guide development toward meaningful solutions rather than technical achievements alone.

Education and capacity building play crucial roles in future development. Communities need not just access to AI solutions but understanding of how to implement and adapt them effectively. Building local capability helps ensure sustainable implementation of AI solutions while enabling communities to guide development toward their specific needs.

The promise of AI for social good extends beyond specific applications to fundamental changes in how we address global challenges. The ability to process vast amounts of data, identify complex patterns, and generate novel solutions suggests new possibilities for addressing persistent problems. This potential for transformation drives continued development while maintaining focus on genuine social benefit.

As we conclude our exploration of AI for social good, we see both significant achievement and promising future direction. The combination of technological capability with humanitarian focus creates powerful opportunities for positive change. This potential drives continued development while reminding us of technology's capacity to serve human needs and values.

CHAPTER 14: THE FUTURE OF AI

Throughout this book, we have explored the fundamentals of artificial intelligence, from its basic principles through its current applications and ethical considerations. Now we turn our attention to the future, examining emerging trends and potential developments that will shape AI's continued evolution.

Our journey through artificial intelligence has revealed both remarkable achievements and significant challenges. We've seen how AI systems analyze vast amounts of data, recognize complex patterns, and automate sophisticated tasks. We've examined applications ranging from personal technology to global challenge solutions. This foundation helps us understand both current capabilities and future possibilities.

The pace of AI development continues to accelerate. New capabilities emerge regularly, pushing the boundaries of what artificial intelligence can achieve. Understanding these developments helps prepare for coming changes while maintaining perspective about both opportunities and challenges ahead.

The integration of AI into more aspects of life and society suggests significant changes ahead. From healthcare and education to environmental protection and creative expression, artificial intelligence influences an expanding range of human activities. This growing influence makes understanding future directions crucial for everyone affected by these technologies.

Current trends in AI development reveal patterns that help indicate future directions. The democratization of AI technology makes these capabilities available to broader audiences. Advances in generative AI open new possibilities for creative expression. Integration of AI with robotics creates novel applications across various industries.

These developments build upon fundamental technologies while suggesting new possibilities. Machine learning continues to advance, enabling more sophisticated analysis and prediction. Neural networks grow more capable, tackling increasingly complex tasks. Natural language processing achieves greater understanding of human communication.

The convergence of different technologies creates possibilities that extend beyond individual capabilities. When AI combines with robotics, new applications emerge in manufacturing and healthcare. Integration with internet-connected devices enables more responsive and adaptive systems. Combining AI technology with specialized sensors creates new monitoring and analysis capabilities.

Understanding these trends helps us prepare for future developments while maintaining realistic expectations about what proves possible. While some predictions about AI development may seem dramatic, careful attention to current trends and fundamental capabilities helps distinguish likely developments from speculation.

Several key trends currently drive innovation in artificial intelligence, shaping both its development and adoption. Understanding these drivers helps reveal likely directions for future advancement while indicating how AI might affect different aspects of society.

The growing accessibility of AI technology represents one of the most significant current trends. Major technology companies now offer platforms that enable individuals and organizations to create AI applications without extensive technical expertise. These "low-code" or "no-code" solutions make AI capabilities available to a much broader audience than previously possible.

This democratization creates new opportunities for innovation across various fields. Healthcare professionals can develop specialized diagnostic tools. Educators can create personalized learning systems. Small businesses can implement sophisticated customer service solutions. This broader participation in AI development brings fresh perspectives and novel applications.

The impact extends beyond traditional technology sectors. As barriers to AI implementation lower, organizations in fields from agriculture to the arts find ways to apply these capabilities to their specific challenges. This expansion of AI application helps drive both technical advancement and practical innovation.

Artificial intelligence increasingly demonstrates capabilities in creative domains. Generative AI systems create text, images, music, and other content with growing sophistication. These developments challenge traditional understanding of creativity while suggesting new possibilities for human-AI collaboration.

The evolution of language models enables increasingly natural text generation. Systems can write everything from business documents to creative fiction with growing capability. While these systems don't truly understand language in human terms, their ability to generate coherent and contextually appropriate text creates new possibilities for content creation and communication.

Visual AI demonstrates similar advancement in creative capabilities. Systems can generate, modify, and combine

179

images in increasingly sophisticated ways. These capabilities suggest new tools for artists and designers while raising questions about the nature of creativity and artistic expression.

The combination of AI with robotics creates particularly powerful possibilities for innovation. Manufacturing systems demonstrate increasing capability for complex assembly and quality control. Healthcare applications range from surgical assistance to patient care support. Logistics operations benefit from automated warehouse management and delivery systems.

This integration enables robots to handle increasingly sophisticated tasks. Rather than following fixed programs, these systems can adapt to changing conditions and learn from experience. This flexibility makes them valuable for complex operations requiring both physical capability and decision-making ability.

The workplace implications of this integration continue to evolve. Rather than simple replacement of human workers, many applications focus on collaboration between humans and AI-powered systems. This cooperation suggests future workplaces where human and artificial capabilities complement each other effectively.

The future of healthcare demonstrates particularly significant potential for AI advancement. Current developments suggest fundamental changes in how healthcare services are delivered and managed, with implications for both medical professionals and patients.

Personalized medicine represents one of the most promising directions for healthcare AI. Systems analyzing individual genetic information, medical history, lifestyle factors, and environmental conditions help tailor treatments to specific patients. This customization improves treatment effectiveness while potentially reducing adverse effects.

Diagnostic capabilities continue to advance through AI application. Systems already demonstrate remarkable accuracy in analyzing medical images for signs of disease. Future developments suggest even greater capability for early detection and accurate diagnosis. The combination of various data sources might enable prediction of health issues before traditional symptoms appear.

Treatment planning benefits from AI's ability to analyze vast amounts of medical research and clinical data. Systems can identify treatment options most likely to succeed for particular patients based on analysis of similar cases and outcomes. This capability helps medical professionals make more informed decisions while considering additional potential options.

The integration of AI throughout healthcare systems creates opportunities for improved service delivery. From appointment scheduling to resource management, automated systems help healthcare facilities operate more efficiently. This optimization helps improve access to care while managing costs effectively.

Telemedicine capabilities continue to evolve through AI enhancement. Remote diagnosis and monitoring systems become more sophisticated, enabling better healthcare delivery to underserved areas. These capabilities prove particularly valuable for managing chronic conditions and providing preventive care.

The combination of various healthcare AI applications suggests more comprehensive approaches to patient care. Systems monitoring individual health data might coordinate with treatment planning systems and healthcare delivery networks. This integration could enable more proactive and coordinated healthcare approaches.

The role of healthcare professionals continues to evolve alongside these technological developments. Rather than replacing medical experts, AI systems increasingly serve as powerful tools supporting professional judgment and expertise. This partnership between human insight and artificial intelligence capabilities suggests more effective future healthcare delivery.

While current trends indicate likely near-term developments in artificial intelligence, longer-term possibilities suggest more fundamental changes. Understanding both immediate directions and potential future developments helps prepare for continued evolution of AI technology.

The concept of Artificial General Intelligence (AGI) represents one of the most significant potential developments in the field. Unlike current AI systems that excel at specific tasks, AGI would demonstrate human-like ability to understand, learn, and apply knowledge across different domains. While this capability remains theoretical, research continues toward this goal.

Current progress toward AGI focuses on developing more flexible and adaptable AI systems. Advances in neural networks and machine learning suggest possibilities for creating systems with broader capabilities. However, significant challenges remain in achieving true general intelligence comparable to human cognitive abilities.

The implications of potential AGI development extend far beyond technical achievement. Such systems might transform numerous aspects of society, from scientific research to creative endeavors. This potential for fundamental change makes understanding AGI development crucial, even while maintaining realistic perspectives about current capabilities and challenges.

The application of AI to global challenges represents another crucial direction for future development. Climate change, resource management, and other complex issues require sophisticated analysis and coordinated responses. Advanced AI systems might help address these challenges more effectively.

Environmental protection demonstrates particular potential for AI application. Future systems might combine various data sources to better understand and predict environmental changes. This capability could enable more effective responses to climate change while supporting conservation efforts and resource management.

Social challenges present another area for potential AI contribution. From education access to economic development, future AI applications might help address persistent social issues. The ability to analyze complex social systems while coordinating responses could support more effective approaches to these challenges.

The evolution of AI capabilities suggests new possibilities for addressing previously intractable problems. The combination of increased processing power, better algorithms, and more sophisticated analysis might enable novel solutions to long-standing challenges. However, success requires careful attention to both technical capabilities and human factors.

As artificial intelligence capabilities continue to advance, ethical considerations become increasingly crucial. Future developments must balance technological possibility with moral responsibility and societal benefit.

The evolution of AI technology requires corresponding development of ethical frameworks. Current principles of responsible AI development provide foundation for future guidance, but advancing capabilities will likely present novel ethical challenges. Frameworks must adapt while maintaining focus on human welfare and societal benefit.

Safety considerations take on particular importance as AI systems become more sophisticated. Current concerns about bias and fairness may evolve into broader questions about system autonomy and decision-making authority. Establishing appropriate boundaries for AI capability and application becomes increasingly crucial as technology advances.

Transparency requirements may need enhancement as systems grow more complex. Current approaches to explaining AI decisions might prove insufficient for more sophisticated future applications. New methods for understanding and validating AI behavior may become necessary for maintaining appropriate oversight and accountability.

The integration of AI into more aspects of society suggests significant social changes ahead. Work environments will likely continue evolving as AI capabilities expand. Educational systems may require adaptation to prepare people for changing technological environments. Social structures may shift as AI influences more aspects of daily life.

Privacy considerations take on new dimensions with advancing AI capability. Current concerns about data collection and usage may evolve as systems develop more sophisticated analysis capabilities. Society may need new approaches to protect individual privacy while enabling beneficial AI applications.

Economic implications of continued AI development require careful consideration. Job displacement concerns may require new approaches to education and employment. Economic systems may need adaptation to ensure benefits of AI advancement are shared appropriately across society.

The balance between innovation and protection becomes increasingly important as capabilities advance. Society must find ways to encourage beneficial AI development while preventing potential harm. This balance requires ongoing dialogue between technologists, ethicists, policymakers, and the public.

As we conclude our exploration of artificial intelligence, we find ourselves at an exciting moment in technological history. The developments we've examined throughout this book represent not just current capabilities but steppingstones toward future possibilities.

The integration of AI into daily life continues to deepen and expand. From personal devices to public infrastructure, artificial intelligence increasingly influences how we live and work. This integration suggests not just technological change but evolution in how we interact with our environment and each other.

Smart homes grow more sophisticated in anticipating and responding to occupant needs. Transportation systems become more efficient at moving people and goods. Educational systems adapt more effectively to individual learning styles. Healthcare delivery becomes more personalized and preventive. Each advancement suggests further possibilities for enhancing human capability and experience.

The workplace continues its transformation through AI integration. Rather than simple automation, we see evolution toward human-AI collaboration. This partnership between human insight and artificial intelligence capabilities suggests new ways of working and creating value. Understanding these changes helps prepare for future opportunities while managing potential challenges.

The journey of artificial intelligence development continues beyond the foundations we've explored in this book. Technical capabilities will advance, creating new possibilities while raising new questions. Society will adapt to these changes while working to ensure technology serves human needs and values.

Education takes on particular importance as AI continues to evolve. Understanding these technologies helps people participate in shaping their development and application. Technical knowledge and ethical awareness are essential in order to foster responsible advancement. This understanding helps ensure artificial intelligence serves as a tool for human benefit rather than a force that controls human experience.

The future of AI depends not just on technical capability but on human wisdom in its development and application. The choices we make about how to develop and deploy these technologies will shape their impact on society. This responsibility requires careful consideration of both possibilities and implications as we move forward.

As we complete our exploration of AI basics, remember that this field continues to evolve. The foundations we've examined provide a framework for understanding future developments. I hope this knowledge will guide you in evaluating and engaging with artificial intelligence as it continues to shape our future.

PREVIEW OF BOOK TWO, *AI TOOLBOX: EMPOWERING THE LEARNER*

Having established a strong foundation in AI fundamentals, our journey continues with an exploration of practical implementation. The second book in the *NewBits AI Trilogy* focuses on empowering you to work effectively with AI technologies, moving from understanding to application.

AI Toolbox: Empowering the Learner guides you through the practical landscape of artificial intelligence. We begin by examining the various types of AI solutions available today, from models and tools to comprehensive platforms. This understanding helps you navigate the growing ecosystem of AI technologies effectively.

The journey then explores specific domains of AI application. We examine language AI solutions that process and generate human language, data AI tools that analyze and derive insights from information, and audio/vision AI systems that work with sound and images. Each domain reveals unique capabilities and applications while building practical understanding of AI implementation.

Specialized applications receive particular attention. We explore how AI transforms healthcare through diagnostic and treatment tools, how robotics AI enables new capabilities in automation and interaction, and how gaming AI creates more engaging and responsive experiences. These practical examples demonstrate AI's impact across different fields.

The book progresses to hands-on development, examining how to combine different AI solutions into comprehensive projects. We explore common development challenges and their solutions, helping you prepare for real-world AI implementation. This practical guidance helps bridge the gap between understanding and application.

Looking forward, we examine emerging trends in AI development and application. This forward-looking perspective helps prepare you for continuing evolution in AI capabilities while maintaining practical focus on current implementation.

Throughout AI Toolbox, the emphasis remains on practical application and empowerment. Each chapter builds your capability to work effectively with AI technologies, moving from basic tool usage to sophisticated solution development. This practical journey builds naturally from the foundations established in this first book while preparing you for actual AI implementation.

I look forward to seeing you in Book Two as you move from understanding AI to implementing these transformative technologies.

AI GLOSSARY: BIT BY BIT

Welcome to the AI Glossary: Bit By Bit. This glossary breaks down essential AI and machine learning terms, from basic data units to advanced concepts. Whether you're new to AI or an expert, the following definitions are provided to illuminate your journey into the world of artificial intelligence.

A

A/B Testing - A method to compare two versions of a model or algorithm by testing them on separate datasets to identify the more effective one.

AI Alignment - Ensuring that AI systems' goals and behaviors align with human values and objectives.

AI Ethics - The study of ethical issues in the design, development, and deployment of AI systems.

AI Model - A mathematical or computational structure that an AI system uses to solve problems or make predictions.

AI Platform - Software that provides tools and environments for developing, training, and deploying AI models.

AI Safety - Research aimed at ensuring that AI systems operate safely and without unintended consequences.

AI System - A combination of hardware and software components used to perform tasks typically requiring human intelligence.

AI Tool - Software or utility that supports AI development, testing, or deployment.

Activation Function - A function used in neural networks to introduce non-linearity, enabling the model to learn from complex patterns.

Active Learning - A machine learning method where the model selectively queries the most informative data points for labeling.

Actor-Critic Model (Reinforcement Learning) - A framework in reinforcement learning where the 'actor' updates policies, and the 'critic' evaluates the action.

Adversarial Attack - A type of attack where inputs are modified to fool AI models into making incorrect predictions.

Adversarial Example - Data that has been intentionally perturbed to cause an AI system to make mistakes.

Algorithm - A set of rules or processes followed in problem-solving or computation, used by AI systems to make decisions.

Anomaly Detection - Identifying patterns or data points that deviate significantly from the norm.

Artificial General Intelligence (AGI) - A form of AI with the ability to understand, learn, and apply intelligence across a broad range of tasks, similar to human intelligence.

Artificial Intelligence (AI) - The simulation of human intelligence by machines, particularly in problem-solving, learning, and decision-making.

Artificial Neural Network (ANN) - A computational model inspired by the way biological neural networks in the human brain process information.

Attention Head (Deep Learning, Transformers) - A component in transformer models that processes input data to focus on relevant aspects for making predictions.

Attention Mechanism - A technique that enables models to focus on specific parts of the input data when making decisions.

Augmented Reality (AR) - An interactive experience where real-world environments are enhanced by computer-generated perceptual information.

Automated Machine Learning (AutoML) - The process of automating the end-to-end process of applying machine learning to real-world problems.

Autonomous - Refers to systems or vehicles capable of making decisions and operating independently without human intervention.

Autonomous Vehicle - A vehicle capable of sensing its environment and navigating without human input, typically using AI systems.

B

BCI (Brain-Computer Interface) - a technology that enables direct communication between the brain and external devices, often using AI to interpret brain signals.

Backpropagation - An algorithm used to calculate gradients in neural networks during the training phase to minimize the error.

Backward Chaining - A reasoning method that starts with a goal and works backward to determine the necessary conditions to achieve that goal.

Batch Normalization (Deep Learning) - A technique that normalizes inputs in a neural network to speed up training and improve performance.

Bayesian Network - A graphical model representing probabilistic relationships among a set of variables.

Bias - Systematic error in AI models, often caused by unbalanced datasets or faulty assumptions.

Bias-Variance Tradeoff (Machine Learning) - The tradeoff between the error introduced by the bias of the model and the variance in the model's predictions.

Big Data - Large datasets that are complex and require advanced methods for processing and analysis.

Biometric AI - AI systems that analyze and interpret biological data, such as fingerprints, facial recognition, or voice recognition.

Bit - The smallest unit of data in computing, represented as 0 or 1.

Bounding Box - A rectangular box used in computer vision to define the location of an object in an image or video.

Byte - A data unit typically consisting of 8 bits, representing a character in computing.

C

C - A general-purpose, procedural computer programming language supporting structured programming.

C# - A modern, object-oriented programming language developed by Microsoft as part of its .NET framework.

C++ - An extension of the C programming language that adds object-oriented features.

CSS (Cascading Style Sheets) - A style sheet language used for describing the presentation of a document written in HTML or XML.

Capsule Network (ANN, Deep Learning) - A type of neural network designed to handle complex hierarchical relationships more effectively than traditional convolutional networks.

Central Processing Unit (CPU) - The primary component of a computer responsible for executing instructions from programs. In AI, the CPU handles general-purpose processing tasks and is used in training and running machine learning models, though it is typically slower for parallel tasks compared to GPUs or TPUs.

Chatbot - A program that uses AI to simulate conversations with users, often used in customer service or personal assistants.

Classification - The process of categorizing data into predefined classes.

Clustering - A technique used to group similar data points together based on certain features.

Cognitive Computing - AI systems that aim to mimic human cognitive functions such as reasoning and learning.

Computer Vision - A field of AI that enables machines to interpret and make decisions based on visual data.

Computer-Generated Imagery (CGI) - The use of AI and other technologies to create images and animations for media and entertainment.

Convergence (Optimization in ML) - The point during optimization when the model parameters stop changing significantly and the learning process stabilizes.

Convolutional Neural Network (CNN) - A deep learning algorithm commonly used in image recognition and processing tasks.

Cross-Entropy Loss (Loss Function) - A loss function commonly used in classification tasks, measuring the difference between predicted probabilities and actual labels.

Cross-validation - A technique for assessing how a machine learning model will generalize to an independent dataset by partitioning the data into training and testing sets.

Crowdsourcing (Data Collection) - The practice of outsourcing tasks, such as data labeling, to a large group of people or the public.

D

Data Augmentation - A technique to increase the diversity of a training dataset by applying random transformations to the data.

Data Drift - Changes in data distributions over time that can negatively affect model performance.

Data Governance - The set of policies and procedures that manage the availability, integrity, security, and usability of data in an organization. In AI, strong data governance ensures that data used for training and decision-making is reliable, secure, and compliant with relevant laws and standards.

Data Labeling - The process of assigning meaningful labels to raw data for training machine learning models.

Data Mining - The process of discovering patterns and insights from large datasets.

Data Preprocessing - The stage where data is cleaned and transformed before being used to train machine learning models.

Decision Boundary - A surface that separates different classes in a classification problem.

Decision Tree - A supervised learning algorithm used for both classification and regression tasks by splitting data into branches.

Deep Learning - A subset of machine learning that involves neural networks with many layers, enabling models to learn from large datasets.

Deep Q-Network (DQN) (Reinforcement Learning) - A model-free reinforcement learning algorithm combining Q-learning with deep learning.

Deepfake - AI-generated or altered media content (typically video or audio) designed to look and sound realistic.

Dimensionality Reduction - The process of reducing the number of features in a dataset while retaining its essential characteristics.

Dropout (Regularization in Neural Networks) - A technique to prevent overfitting by randomly dropping units from the neural network during training.

E

Edge AI - AI that processes data locally on devices rather than relying on cloud computing, reducing latency.

Embedding - A representation of data in a lower-dimensional space used in machine learning tasks such as NLP.

Embodied AI (Robotics, AI Systems) - AI systems that are

physically integrated into robots or devices, enabling interaction with the physical world.

End-to-End Learning (Neural Networks) - A learning approach where a system is trained directly on the input-output mapping without intermediate steps.

Ensemble Learning - A technique that combines multiple machine learning models to improve performance.

Epoch - A full iteration over the entire dataset during the training phase of a machine learning model.

Evolutionary Algorithm - Optimization algorithms inspired by the process of natural selection.

Exabyte (EB) - A data unit equivalent to 1,024 petabytes.

Expert System - An AI system that mimics the decision-making ability of a human expert.

Explainable AI (XAI) - AI systems designed to provide human-understandable explanations for their decisions and outputs.

F

Feature Engineering - The process of selecting, modifying, and creating features for improving machine learning models.

Feature Extraction - The process of transforming raw data into a set of features to be used by a machine learning model.

Federated Learning - A technique where models are trained across multiple devices without sharing raw data, improving privacy.

Few-Shot Learning - A type of machine learning where a model is trained with very few labeled examples.

Fine-tuning - Adjusting the parameters of a pre-trained model to apply it to a specific task.

Firmware - A specialized type of software that is embedded directly into hardware devices to control their functions. Firmware is typically stored in non-volatile memory and manages the basic operations of hardware, including devices used in AI systems, such as sensors and robotics.

Flask - A lightweight Python web application framework.

Fuzzy Logic - A form of logic used in AI that allows reasoning with uncertain or approximate values, rather than precise ones.

G

Generative AI - AI systems capable of generating new data, such as images, text, or music, that resemble human-created content.

Generative Adversarial Network (GAN) - A model consisting of two networks, a generator and a discriminator, that learn together to generate realistic data.

Genetic Algorithm - An optimization algorithm based on principles of natural selection and genetics.

Gigabyte (GB) - A unit of data equivalent to 1,024 megabytes.

Gradient Clipping (Optimization in Deep Learning) - A technique used to prevent exploding gradients during the training of neural networks.

Gradient Descent - An optimization algorithm used to minimize a loss function by iteratively moving in the direction of the steepest descent.

Graph Neural Network - A type of neural network that directly operates on graph structures, enabling learning on data that is structured as graphs.

Graphics Processing Unit (GPU) - A specialized processor designed for parallel processing tasks, originally used for rendering graphics. In AI, GPUs are widely used for training deep learning models due to their ability to handle multiple computations simultaneously, significantly speeding up the training process.

H

HTML (Hypertext Markup Language) - The standard markup language for creating web pages and web applications.

Hallucination (in AI) - When an AI model generates output (such as a response or image) that is factually incorrect or nonsensical.

Hardware - The physical components of a computer or device that perform computational tasks. In AI, hardware includes processors (like CPUs, GPUs, TPUs), storage, sensors, and other equipment that provides the computational power needed to train models and execute AI algorithms.

Heuristic - A problem-solving approach that uses practical methods or rules of thumb for making decisions.

Hybrid AI - Systems combining symbolic reasoning and neural networks to leverage the strengths of both approaches.

Hyperparameter - Parameters in machine learning models that are set before training and not learned from the data.

Hyperparameter Tuning - The process of adjusting hyperparameters to optimize the performance of a machine learning model.

I

Imbalanced Dataset - A dataset where some classes are significantly over- or under-represented, which can affect model performance.

Inference - The process of making predictions using a trained machine learning model.

Interpretable Machine Learning (IML) - Techniques that enable understanding and explaining how machine learning models make decisions.

J

JavaScript - A high-level, interpreted programming language that is a core technology of the World Wide Web.

K

K-Means Clustering - A clustering algorithm that partitions data into K distinct groups based on similarity.

K-Nearest Neighbors (KNN) - A machine learning algorithm that classifies data points based on the closest labeled examples in the dataset.

Kernel Method - Techniques in machine learning that use a kernel function to enable algorithms to operate in a high-dimensional space.

Kilobyte (KB) - A data unit equivalent to 1,024 bytes.

Knowledge Base - A structured database of information used to support AI systems, such as expert systems.

Knowledge Distillation - A technique in which a smaller model is trained to replicate the behavior of a larger, more complex model.

L

Large Language Model (LLM) - A deep learning model trained on vast amounts of text data to understand and generate human-like text.

Learning Rate (Gradient Descent) - A hyperparameter that determines the step size for updating weights in gradient-based optimization.

Long Short-Term Memory (LSTM) - A type of recurrent neural network capable of learning long-term dependencies in sequential data.

Loss Function (Optimization) - A function used to measure the error or difference between the predicted output of a model and the actual outcome.

M

Machine Learning (ML) - A subset of AI that involves systems learning patterns from data and improving over time without being explicitly programmed.

Machine Learning Operations (MLOps) - A set of practices for deploying, managing, and monitoring machine learning models in production.

Markov Decision Process (MDP) (Reinforcement Learning) - A framework for modeling decision-making where outcomes are partly random and partly under the control of an agent.

Megabyte (MB) - A data unit equivalent to 1,024 kilobytes.

Meta-Learning - A machine learning approach where models learn how to learn, improving their adaptability to new tasks.

Model - A mathematical representation of a system, process, or behavior that can make predictions or decisions based on input data.

Model Compression - Techniques to reduce the size and complexity of machine learning models while maintaining performance.

Monte Carlo Method (Statistical Learning) - A computational algorithm that uses random sampling to solve problems that might be deterministic in principle.

Multi-Agent System - A system composed of multiple interacting intelligent agents that work together or compete to achieve goals.

Multi-Task Learning - A machine learning approach where a model is trained on multiple related tasks simultaneously, sharing knowledge across tasks.

MySQL - An open-source relational database management system that uses Structured Query Language (SQL).

N

Natural Language Generation (NLG) - The use of AI to generate human-like language based on structured data or inputs.

Natural Language Processing (NLP) - A field of AI that focuses on the interaction between computers and human language.

Natural Language Understanding (NLU) - A subfield of NLP focused on understanding the meaning and context of human language.

Neural Architecture Search - The process of automating the design of neural network architectures using machine learning.

Neural Tangent Kernel (Theoretical ML) - A theoretical

framework for understanding the behavior of neural networks during training.

Neurosymbolic AI - An approach combining neural networks and symbolic reasoning to enhance the interpretability of AI systems.

Node.js - An open-source, cross-platform JavaScript runtime environment that executes JavaScript code outside of a web browser.

Noisy Student (Data Augmentation) - A technique that improves the accuracy of models by training them on both labeled and noisy augmented data.

O

One-Shot Learning - A form of learning where a model can recognize new objects or patterns after being trained on a single example.

Ontology - A structured representation of knowledge and concepts used in AI for reasoning about relationships and entities.

Open Source - Software or models made available with a license that allows anyone to view, modify, and distribute the source code. Open-source AI tools are often free to use, though they may have associated costs for implementation or support. These tools promote collaboration and transparency in the development of AI technologies.

Optimizer (Deep Learning) - Algorithms or methods used to minimize the loss function and improve the accuracy of a model during training.

Overfitting - A scenario where a machine learning model learns too closely from training data, performing poorly on unseen data.

P

PHP - A server-side scripting language designed for web development.

Parameter - Variables in a machine learning model that are

learned from data during training, such as weights in a neural network.

Pattern Recognition - The ability of AI models to recognize patterns or regularities in data.

Perceptron - The simplest type of artificial neural network, primarily used in binary classification tasks.

Permutation Importance - A technique for measuring the importance of features in a machine learning model by evaluating the change in model performance after shuffling each feature.

Petabyte (PB) - A unit of data equal to 1,024 terabytes.

Predictive Analytics - Using statistical techniques and machine learning to predict future outcomes based on historical data.

Preprocessing - Preparing and transforming raw data into a suitable format for training machine learning models.

Proprietary - Software, models, or systems that are owned by a company or individual and have restrictions on access, usage, and modification. Proprietary AI tools may require a license or payment to use and are typically closed to public modification and distribution. Access is often limited based on a pay-to-use model, though some proprietary tools may offer free tiers with limited functionality.

Pruning - A technique to reduce the size of a neural network by eliminating weights or neurons that contribute little to model accuracy.

Python - A high-level, interpreted programming language known for its simplicity and readability, widely used in AI, data science, and web development.

Q

Quantum Computing - A type of computing that leverages quantum mechanics to perform calculations at exponentially faster rates than classical computers.

R

Random Forest (Ensemble Learning) - An ensemble learning technique that uses multiple decision trees to improve prediction accuracy.

React - A JavaScript library for building user interfaces, particularly single-page applications.

Recurrent Neural Network (RNN) - A type of neural network designed to handle sequential data such as time series or text.

Regression - A type of supervised learning used to predict continuous outcomes based on input features.

Regularization (Preventing Overfitting) - Techniques used to reduce overfitting by adding constraints to a machine learning model.

Reinforcement Learning - A machine learning paradigm where agents learn to make decisions through rewards and punishments.

Robotics - The use of AI in designing and building machines that can perform tasks typically carried out by humans.

Rule-Based System - AI systems that apply a set of predefined rules to reach conclusions or make decisions.

S

SQL (Structured Query Language) - A standardized language used for managing and manipulating relational databases.

Self-Supervised Learning (Machine Learning) - A learning approach where models learn from unlabeled data by creating their own labels.

Semantic Analysis - The process of understanding the meaning and context of language in AI and NLP tasks.

Sentiment Analysis - An NLP technique used to determine the sentiment (positive, negative, neutral) expressed in text.

Software - Programs and applications that run on hardware to perform specific tasks. In AI, software refers to the code, frameworks, and models that enable data processing, model training, and decision-making. AI software can be proprietary or open-source and may operate on various types of hardware.

Sparsity (ML models) - A concept in machine learning where only a small percentage of features are relevant to the model's output.

Supervised Learning - A type of machine learning where the model is trained on labeled data, learning to predict output based on input features.

Support Vector Machine (SVM) - A supervised learning algorithm used for classification and regression tasks by finding the hyperplane that best separates data points.

Swarm Intelligence (Multi-Agent Systems) - A collective behavior of decentralized, self-organized agents used in AI to solve complex problems.

Synthetic Data - Artificially generated data used to train AI models, often used when real-world data is scarce or sensitive.

T

Tensor Processing Unit (TPU) - A specialized hardware accelerator designed by Google specifically for AI and machine learning tasks, particularly for deep learning and neural networks. TPUs are optimized for TensorFlow workloads and offer faster computation than CPUs and GPUs for specific AI tasks, especially in large-scale training.

Terabyte (TB) - A unit of data storage equal to 1,024 gigabytes.

Tokenization (NLP) - The process of breaking text into smaller units, such as words or subwords, for analysis in NLP models.

Transfer Learning - A technique where a pre-trained model is adapted to perform a new, but related, task.

Transformer - A deep learning architecture designed for tasks such as NLP that relies on attention mechanisms to process input data.

Turing Test - A test proposed by Alan Turing to evaluate

a machine's ability to exhibit intelligent behavior indistinguishable from that of a human.

U

UX - Short for User Experience, refers to the design and interaction of users with a product or service, especially important in AI system interfaces.

Unsupervised Learning - A machine learning paradigm where models are trained on unlabeled data to find patterns or structure.

V

Validation Set - A subset of the data used to tune model parameters and avoid overfitting during the training process.

Vector - A mathematical representation of data points in machine learning and deep learning.

Virtual Reality (VR) - The use of computer technology to create simulated, immersive environments.

Voice Recognition - AI technology that identifies and processes human speech for various applications.

W

WordPress - An open-source content management system based on PHP and MySQL.

X

XML (eXtensible Markup Language) - A markup language that defines a set of rules for encoding documents in a format that is both human-readable and machine-readable.

Y

Yottabyte (YB) - The largest standard unit of data storage, equivalent to 1,024 zettabytes.

Z

Zero-Shot Learning (Machine Learning) - A learning approach where the model makes predictions on classes or tasks it has not been explicitly trained on.

Zettabyte (ZB) - A data unit equivalent to 1,024 exabytes.

ABOUT NEWBITS.AI

The newbits.ai ecosystem emerged from a simple yet powerful vision: to demystify artificial intelligence and make this complex technological frontier accessible to everyone. This dynamic learning environment, where learning, discovery, and innovation flourish together, was created by an AI enthusiast and curator, who authored the *NewBits AI Trilogy: AI Basics: The Fundamentals*, *AI Toolbox: Empowering the Learner*, and *AI Frontier: Navigating the Cutting Edge*. This digital nexus, accessible through the internet domain newbits.ai, mirrors the books' mission to bridge the gap between cutting edge AI technology and curious minds at all levels.

At the foundation of newbits.ai stands the *AI Solutions* Marketplace, a carefully curated space where theory meets practical application. Here, visitors discover a rich tapestry of artificial intelligence tools spanning six essential categories: Language, Data, Audio/Vision, Healthcare, Robotics, and Gaming. Within Language, users find natural language processing tools and translation systems. The Data category offers analytics platforms and data management solutions.

Audio/Vision presents solutions for speech recognition, image processing, computer vision, and visualization tools. Healthcare showcases medical imaging and diagnostic innovations. Robotics features autonomous systems and control software, while Gaming presents AI driven development tools and virtual reality platforms.

The marketplace distinguishes between models and tools and platforms, allowing users to focus their search based on their specific needs. Visitors can easily navigate between open source and proprietary solutions, ensuring they find resources that align with their preferences and requirements. Through intuitive browsing and filtering options, users can refine their search by category, solution type, and featured solutions, transforming what could be an overwhelming journey into a streamlined discovery process.

Each listing offers detailed insights and community reviews, ensuring that whether someone is taking their first steps into AI implementation or seeking advanced platforms for complex projects, they can make informed decisions with confidence.

Beyond the marketplace lies the *AI Hub*, a vibrant community space that pulses with the energy of shared discovery. This dynamic network spans across nine distinct platforms: Reddit, YouTube, Spotify, Facebook, X (formerly Twitter), LinkedIn, Medium, Quora, and Discord. Through thoughtful discussions on Reddit, engaging content on YouTube and Spotify, industry insights on LinkedIn, enriching articles on Medium, knowledge sharing on Quora, community building on Facebook, and real time exchanges on Discord and X, the Hub weaves together a tapestry of knowledge where every voice contributes to our collective understanding. Here, beginners find mentorship, experts share insights, and innovations spark from the collision of curious minds.

The *AI Ed* page serves as the gateway to our signature educational content, featuring the podcast series *AI Ed: From*

Bits to Breakthroughs. Here, visitors can access a carefully structured journey that mirrors the natural progression of learning found in our book trilogy. The series begins with foundational concepts in *AI Basics: The Fundamentals*, advances through practical applications in *AI Toolbox: Empowering the Learner*, and ultimately explores the cutting edge of possibility in *AI Frontier: Navigating the Cutting Edge*. Each episode builds upon the last, creating a comprehensive narrative that guides listeners from their first encounter with artificial intelligence through to the most advanced concepts shaping our future.

Supporting this educational journey, the *AI Glossary: Bit by Bit* serves as a trusted companion, illuminating the path from basic terminology to complex concepts. This carefully crafted resource grows alongside our community, ensuring that the language of artificial intelligence remains accessible to all who wish to learn.

Together, these elements form something greater than their individual parts, standing as a testament to the power of accessible education, community collaboration, and practical implementation. Just as the book trilogy illuminates the path from fundamental concepts to cutting edge innovations, newbits.ai represents an unwavering commitment to transforming the complex world of artificial intelligence into a journey of discovery that anyone can undertake. As artificial intelligence continues to reshape our world, this commitment ensures that everyone has the opportunity to understand, implement, and innovate in this revolutionary field.

In the end, newbits.ai embodies a simple truth: that the future of artificial intelligence belongs not to a select few, but to everyone who dares to learn, to explore, and to imagine. Through educational content, community engagement, and comprehensive resources, the mission of demystifying AI continues, making the complex simple and the cutting edge accessible. After all, in this rapidly evolving landscape, every bit of knowledge counts, but none more so than the new bits that light the way forward.

GIL OREN

OUR NAME: NEWBITS.AI

Names tell stories. They carry meaning, purpose, and vision. In the realm of artificial intelligence, where complex concepts meet practical applications, a name must bridge the gap between technical precision and accessible understanding. The story of newbits.ai begins with this bridge, connecting the foundational elements of digital technology with the transformative potential of human learning.

At the heart of every digital innovation lies a fundamental unit of information: the bit. This binary digit, capable of being either zero or one, forms the foundation of our name and reflects our mission in the world of artificial intelligence. To understand newbits.ai is to understand how the smallest unit of digital information scales to enable the vast possibilities of modern computing and artificial intelligence.

A bit, in its simplest form, acts like a tiny switch, either off or on. When eight bits come together, they form a byte, capable of representing a single character like a letter or number. As bits and bytes combine, they create progressively larger units that power the digital world we interact with every day:

Unit	Approximate Value	Real-World Example
Bit	Single binary value (0 or 1)	The smallest piece of data in computing
Byte	8 bits	A single character (e.g. 'A' or '5')
Kilobyte	1,024 bytes	A text document, simple email, or basic app
Megabyte	1,024 kilobytes	A high-resolution photo, MP3 song, or standard mobile app
Gigabyte	1,024 megabytes	A movie, complex app, or smartphone storage capacity
Terabyte	1,024 gigabytes	External hard drive, large data backups, or server storage
Petabyte	1,024 terabytes	Data centers, cloud storage providers, or large-scale AI datasets
Exabyte	1,024 petabytes	Total data generated globally in a year
Zettabyte	1,024 exabytes	Global data storage capacity
Yottabyte	1,024 zettabytes	Theoretical future data scale

In daily life, these units manifest in familiar ways. A simple text file or short email might occupy a few kilobytes. A high-quality photo, MP3 song, or standard mobile app typically requires several megabytes. Movies, complex applications, and smartphone storage capacities are measured in gigabytes. Large storage devices like external hard drives often hold terabytes of data. Data centers and major cloud providers work with petabytes, while units like exabytes, zettabytes, and yottabytes represent the immense scale of global data storage and future possibilities.

In terms of data transmission, these units determine the speed at which information travels across networks, measured in bits per second (bps). Internet speeds, typically measured in megabits per second, reflect how quickly data can be downloaded or uploaded, directly affecting everything from streaming videos to downloading applications.

The name newbits.ai carries this symbolism in each of its elements. "New" represents the constant evolution and innovation in artificial intelligence, acknowledging that yesterday's cutting edge becomes tomorrow's foundation. "Bits" holds dual significance, representing both the fundamental units of digital information and the incremental pieces of knowledge that accumulate to create understanding. The ".ai" domain extension definitively anchors our identity in artificial intelligence, declaring our dedicated focus on this transformative field.

Just as bits scale from simple binary values to the massive datasets that power modern artificial intelligence, newbits.ai scales from fundamental concepts to advanced applications. Through the *AI Solutions* Marketplace, each tool and platform represents countless bits working in harmony. In the *AI Hub*, every shared insight adds new bits of knowledge to our collective understanding. The *AI Ed* podcast series and *AI Glossary* transform complex concepts into accessible bits of learning, while this book trilogy guides readers through their journey from basic bits to breakthrough insights.

This scalability of bits, from foundational elements to complex systems, embodies the accessibility championed by newbits.ai. The phrase coined by the author, "It's all about the bits, especially the new bits," echoes through every aspect of artificial intelligence, celebrating both the technical foundation of digital innovation and the journey of continuous learning that defines the AI frontier. Each new bit of knowledge, like each binary digit in a computer system, builds upon what came before, creating ever greater possibilities for understanding, innovation, and discovery.

From the smallest bit to the largest dataset, from the first step into artificial intelligence to mastery of advanced concepts, the name newbits.ai captures the essence of digital evolution and perpetual learning in this revolutionary field.

GIL OREN

EXTENDED DEDICATIONS

I dedicate this book to my family. To my extraordinary wife, Melissa, and my incredible children, Zachary, Sydney, and Ava. And, of course, our adopted family member, our incessantly loving, and always hungry canine, Dixie.

Melissa, you have been my life since the moment I first saw you, and you have always been by my side, the wind in my sails, and my inspiration no matter the challenges and obstacles life has thrown my way. You are kind, loving, compassionate, keenly observant, and one of the world's best listeners, which is why so many others, myself included, seek your advice. You are also an exceptional mother to our amazing children, and often times, more often than you signed up for, that applies not only to our children. You are a godsend to us all and the bedrock of our family.

Zachary, Sydney and Ava, I am so proud of all three of you.

Zachary, you are a Rockstar. You are a well-rounded, hardworking, engaging, and brilliant young adult. You plan your work, and you work your plan to perfection. At the same time, you find room for family, friends and good times. You have managed to master the balance of, "work like a captain and party like a pirate." I enjoy nothing more than times with you engaging about sports or debating world politics. Watching you play golf is not bad either.

Sydney, you make the world smile. You bring dedication to excellence in all you do. From your academic endeavors to your countless accomplishments in the classroom and in the world of athletics, you are truly sensational. That said, your most admirable asset is your heart. Your kind spirit is unmatched, and it is what everyone that is privileged to know you, meet you, or even see you for a fleeting moment, feels. That is your superpower. And, you are hilarious too, which is a gift. I cherished every moment of watching you play lacrosse and basketball. And, of course, I always look forward to watching old comedies with you, or simply rocking weird with you. Which is why you are my So Funny.

Ava, you light up the world. Your spirit is infectious, and I often find myself trying to figure out who are all of these people that circle your planet. You are the orchestrator in our home and have been ever since you could talk. You are the most observant person I know, and you fiercely defend those whom you covet. These attributes are precious blessings, but let's not forget your exceptional athletic skills, social skills and gifted style. Ava, I feel good whenever I am around you, and that is a rare power indeed.

I look forward to watching the three of you write the future chapters of your stories, and I appreciate all of you more than the world turns. You are my world.

ABOUT THE AUTHOR

Gil Oren is a business strategist, critical thinker, and serial entrepreneur whose fascination with artificial intelligence led to the creation of the *NewBits AI Trilogy*. With over two decades of experience navigating complex business challenges, he offers a unique perspective on understanding and explaining AI technology.

Gil's academic and professional journey spans multiple domains, including law, real estate development, private equity, intellectual property, research and development, manufacturing, marketing, distribution, sales, and sustainability. This diverse background gives him a comprehensive understanding of various industries, enhancing his ability to relate AI concepts to different sectors effectively.

In the chemical industry, Gil developed, patented, and deployed novel technologies, showcasing his capacity for innovation and practical application of complex ideas. This hands-on experience with technological advancement provides him with deep insights into the potential and challenges of adopting transformative technologies like artificial intelligence.

He has collaborated with a wide range of organizations, from startups and Fortune 100 companies to nation-states and the armed forces. Leading an organization conducting business across the Americas, Europe, Australia, the Middle East, and Asia has given him a global perspective on the technological and cultural challenges that come with implementing new technologies. This global experience enables him to address AI's impact on a worldwide scale, making his insights valuable to an international audience.

As an Executive Chairman and Board Member, Gil has gained profound understanding of strategic technology implementation and governance. His legal expertise as a licensed attorney in the State of Florida and the District of Columbia equips him with unique insights into the practical and regulatory aspects of technology adoption. This combination of strategic and legal knowledge strengthens his ability to guide readers through the complexities of AI integration in business.

Motivated by the desire to demystify artificial intelligence, Gil is committed to making this transformative technology accessible to everyone. In the *NewBits AI Trilogy*, he addresses the intimidating aspects of AI, breaking down complex concepts to help readers understand and navigate the AI landscape effectively.

When not exploring artificial intelligence and emerging technologies, Gil enjoys spending time with family and friends, playing piano and guitar, and following collegiate and professional sports.

He firmly believes that relationships and teamwork are fundamental to achieving success in life and in business.